# The Digital Image

# The Digital Image

### Ron Graham
PhD, CPhys, FInstP, AMRAeS

Whittles Publishing

CRC PRESS

Typeset by
Compuscript Ltd., Shannon, Ireland

Published by
**Whittles Publishing Ltd.,**
Dunbeath Mains Cottages,
Dunbeath
Caithness, KW6 6EY
Scotland, UK
www.whittlespublishing.com

Distributed in North America by
**CRC Press LLC,**
Taylor and Francis Group,
6000 Broken Sound Parkway NW,
Suite 300,
Boca Raton, FL 33487, USA

© 2005 R. Graham

ISBN 1-904445-00-4
USA ISBN 0-8493-9569-0

Printed by Bell and Bain Ltd., Glasgow

*To my wife, Joan,*
*who provided the necessary encouragement and support*
*that made this book possible*

# Preface to Second Edition

When I started on the first edition of this book there were approximately 40 different digital cameras on the market; that was eight years ago. One year later we could count nearly 200 digital cameras of all types, but now the industry has grown and we have about 3000 digital cameras devoted mainly to the amateur market. The digital camera is now well established and cameras of 3MPx and more are commonplace for the amateur. The popularity of these cameras is due in particular to the ever-decreasing prices; a 3MPx outfit costing £100 or less. The salient feature of the digital market is the time factor: no sooner is a product in the shops than it is overtaken by yet another product, and one may find difficulty in getting a camera that is only a few months old. The digital camera has a number of prices, depending on its age (in months from first appearance), so beware!

*The Digital Image* remains a general text that includes something for everyone. It is written for students, lecturers, professionals and amateurs – in fact all who wish to engage with this new and rapidly expanding technology. The early chapters comprise an introduction to imaging and cover the topics of optics, electronics and photography as required for this subject. Information on semiconductor technology then follows, as the basis for major chapters on digital cameras and image processing, with additional material on digital printers. The book concludes with numerous examples of digital imaging applications, ranging from press and commercial photography to military applications, aerial survey and astronomy.

Returning to the matter of prices, the cheapest camera currently available (2005) is the Praktica Micropix with 0.1M effective pixels (352 × 288) and a 16 Mb internal memory that can capture 80 images, priced at £15. The Praktica Slimpix, priced at £25, provides 0.3M effective pixels (640 × 480) and 64 Mb of internal memory plus an LCD status panel. The images, however, are only suitable for email attachments or for posting on the web. It is interesting to note that the Kodak DC-40 of 1996 cost £720 and had a chip of 760 × 512 pixels, little better than the Praktica Slimpix which owes its cheapness to the advances in CMOS technology over the past nine years.

These modest pixel cameras are good for recording items where quality is of little importance. For the person who wants to emulate film at the 6 × 4 inch print size, something a little more impressive is required. There are many cameras today which sport a 1.3 MPx (1280 × 960) chip at around £50, such as the Shotz Mini Shotz with 1.3M effective pixels and 16 Mb internal memory. The Nikon Coolpix 2200 has 2.0M effective pixels (1600 × 1200) and can certainly be classed as a good amateur camera, with 14.5 Mb internal memory at a modest £90. Then we go to the 3.2 Mpx cameras, such as the Praktica DCZ-3.4 with 3.2M effective pixels (2048 × 1536) priced at £100. The Jenoptik JD 4.1 has 4.0M effective pixels (2272 × 1704) and costs the same as the Praktica DCZ. Built for the more serious amateur is the Samsung Digimax 430, with 4.0M effective pixels (2272 × 1704) and a 32 Mb SD card priced £150. The Samsung Digimax A5, with 5.0M effective pixels (2560 × 1920), brings the cost of near professional quality down to £200.

Digital cameras suitable for the professional include the Fujifilm Finepix S7000 with 6.3M effective pixels (2848 × 2136) costing £350. These six million pixel cameras are certainly as good as any film camera, and can produce results suitable for any kind of work. The Olympus C-8080 Wide Zoom has 8.0M effective pixels (3264 × 2448) and a movie recording function with sound and has a price tag of £550. Digital cameras such as the Kodak 420 CIR (colour infrared), the CIR option being especially useful in the forensic science and mapping fields, have been long outdated due to an effective pixel size of only 1.54M. Similarly, the Kodak 460 CIR of 6.1M was very useful in these fields, particularly with its 18 × 28 mm format, but owing to its price (£21,000) and limited sales it was discontinued in 2000.

Since early 2001 we have had a great breakthrough with chips that were 16 MPx in size, namely the Kodak DCS Pro Back, which is a 16 MPx CCD sensor (with the usual Kodak pixel size of 9 mm square) of 4080 × 4080 pixels, and an array of Indium Tin Oxide (ITO). The Pro Back can be fitted to cameras such as the Hasselblad 555ELD, or the Mamiya RZ67 Pro II. The chip size is 36.65 mm square, and with the Hasselblad can be used with the excellent Zeiss Distagon 40 mm $f/4$ lens making it a perfect combination for medium format aerial photography. Image capture is 17 Mb which is interpolated (Bayer pattern) to 48 Mb in RGB colour. The price is around £13,000 complete with Hasselblad 555EL.

Digital imagery employs the technology of CCD (charge coupled device) that has been with us for more than 30 years and shows no signs of becoming outdated. Yet in the background and now rapidly closing on CCD is CMOS (complementary metal oxide semiconductor) technology with commercial examples now in production. Foveon X3, a CMOS based sensor that does without the usual colour filter array (CFA) such as the well-known Bayer filter, records each of the RGB colours in depth. An SLR camera, the Sigma SD 9, has been produced using this technology that increases the pixel resolution by a factor of three.

Above all, digital imagery offers much more flexibility than film. Access to an image without the inconvenience of a darkroom, water or chemicals is certainly foremost, but there is also the speed of access via the computer, the scope for image manipulation and the possibility of sending an image around the world via the internet.

Ron Graham
PhD, CPhys, FInstP, AMRAeS

# Acknowledgements

I should like to express my appreciation to Alexander Koh, RSGIS Unit, Bath Spa University College, for his unstinting help in the preparation of this book. My gratitude also goes to two people who made this second edition possible. To my wife Joan, for her practical assistance with information and records and last, but not least, to my publisher Dr Keith Whittles, for his constant encouragement and valuable advice.

# Contents

# Introduction

The human eye-brain mechanism must represent the ultimate imaging system where, for a given scene, the visual mechanism provides spatial information in three dimensions and full colour.

The visual appreciation of a scene comprises both objective (measurable) and subjective (perceptual) components involving many disciplines including: physics, psychophysics, chemistry, anatomy, physiology and aesthetics.

Early humans strove to record their world by carving crude drawings on stone; and this developed through the ages, by way of materials and skill, with an ever-growing appreciation for perspective, scale and artistic impression. By the mid-nineteenth century photography was well established in monochrome, and by the turn of the twentieth century stereoscopy and colour had also been exploited within the medium. Indeed, stereoscopy was more popular in the nineteenth century than it ever was in the twentieth!

As the quality of photographic materials advanced, in terms of speed (sensitivity to light), spectral sensitivity (embracing radiation from X-rays to the near infrared), spatial resolution (sub-micrometer) and accuracy of representation, so did camera technology.

Until the mid-twentieth century most practical photography was restricted to monochrome and it is interesting to reflect that few people really cared about colour —what they never had they never missed! Monochrome images served very well, and the average person was perfectly content to accept achromatic representations of what they actually saw in full colour. Similarly, the same acceptance was given to two-dimensional representations of a scene, the viewer being content to assume the third dimension from limited visual cues, such as perspective, scale, obscuration, atmosphere, etc. These visual assumptions continue to be accepted today as much as they ever were! And we need look no further than the monochrome images seen in newspapers and journals to appreciate this fact. Even so, only the dedicated amateur photographer will be happy with monochrome these days—colour is the expected norm and its quality is good. Stereoscopy is still available of course (but not a popular option) and although its 'cardboard cut-out' appearance is little more than a historic oddity to most people, it still remains highly important for technical purposes, such as scientific recording, photogrammetry and mapping. Indeed, large format aerial (mapping) photographs are now digitised and viewed on computer monitors via spectacles (softcopy photogrammetry) in much the same way as the old anaglyph and vectograph processes, with all the advantages of computer software to assist in the manufacture of accurate maps.

Since the advent of the laser we have had holography—a system where a truly 'solid' form of imagery can be realised. As one of the earliest practitioners of this technology I employed this medium as a scientific tool where, with its ability to form a three-dimensional image that can be inspected (with full parallax along its entire depth) at leisure, even fast transient events could be recorded for subsequent analysis. Holography remains an important scientific aid and although the detail resolved by a hologram is extremely fine, and requires photographic materials capable of the highest spatial resolution, it is interesting to note that in one significant industrial application, holographic interferometry, digital cameras are now employed to record the low resolution interferometric fringes created on various materials under mechanical, thermal or electrical stress loads.

So, at the start of the twenty-first century, we can justly applaud the many new developments that have occurred in photography and, because of the vast scope of its scientific importance, have made the process invaluable as a diagnostic tool, as well as a graphic form of communication and an exciting medium for artistic expression. Nevertheless, apart from the innate acceptance of a two-dimensional representation of a scene, or object, equally important features, such as parallax (the apparent change in position of an object, or image, due to change in position of the eye of the observer) and viewpoint remain as unchallenged to day as they have ever been. And now, in the final decade of the twentieth century, we have another significant development in photography, but this time it is the medium itself!

The title adopted for this book is 'The Digital Image', but it could equally be 'Digital Photography', or 'Electronic Imagery', and no doubt the reader will have his or her own views regarding the semantics at issue. It could be argued that 'photography' is not an appropriate term for a recording system that employs a CCD (charge coupled device) array rather than chemically produced silver-halide grains. But since (roughly speaking) photography means 'drawing with light', the term surely denies any need to specify the medium employed! As to the use of the word 'electronic' this is equally lacking in any specific discrimination between AgH (silver halide) and the silicon-based MOS (metal oxide semiconductor) used in CCDs, since both sensors activate free electrons under exposure to appropriate radiation!

Purists might argue that, since a CCD or CMOS camera employs an array that directly stores an electronic charge in proportion to image radiation, then the appropriate term should be 'electronic imagery'. But this tends to ignore the most significant aspect of CCD imaging, which is its system compatability with computers! After exposure each cell in the array is 'clocked-out' by the system's electronics so that each CCD (thousands or millions of them) is given a digital code according to its signal strength (image intensity) and $x, y$ position within the array. At this point in the imaging process, the system becomes 'digital' and as such can be stored in the camera—and subsequently downloaded into a computer.

Digital systems have many advantages, and as the manufacturers improve their products it is safe to say that digital cameras will get better, less expensive and more popular, just as their host—the computer has done before them.

Although this book is devoted to digital imagery it cannot satisfactorily address the subject in isolation, that is to say, without reference to the fundamental physics and perceptual phenomena that relate the image to its subject, and to the four basic types of two-dimensional imaging systems. As a consequence, the first part of the book is devoted to basic theory in order to emphasise underlying concepts and to provide a foundation for those without a traditional background in optics or photography.

# 1 Radiometry

Whereas we usually refer to 'light' when dealing with photography, this can be misleading when we discuss radiation below or above the visible spectrum. This is particularly true when dealing with the ultra-violet or infrared. As can be seen from Fig. 1.1, the radiometric spectrum projected by the sun is a continuum extending from high-energy (high-frequency) cosmic and gamma rays, through X-rays and the ultra-violet to the relatively narrow band of visible rays, before extending through the infrared to radio waves.

## 1.1 Electromagnetic Radiation

In Fig. 1.1 we see the entire spectrum of electromagnetic energy which, as the name suggests, exists in the simultaneous form of electricity and magnetism. These two forms of the same energy are transmitted together as electromagnetic radiation (EMR). One cannot exist without the other: a flow of electric current always produces magnetism, and magnetism is used to produce electricity.

EMR is propagated outwards from its source at a velocity ($c$) of 300 000 000 metres per second ($3 \times 10^8$ ms$^{-1}$). Both the electric and magnetic fields are propagated as transverse waves. Wave motion and the transfer of energy are best explained by looking at what happens to water when a stone is thrown into a perfectly calm pool. As the stone enters the water it sets up a disturbance to create waves that eventually reach the edges of the pool. But the particles of water do not move towards the edges of the pool—they simply move up and down. Only the disturbance (energy) moves outwards from the stone—as a series of wavefronts. A wave in which the particles move at right angles to the direction of travel of the wave is called a transverse wave.

Electromagnetic waves have an electrical field ($E$) associated with a magnetic one ($H$) at right angles to it, and both are at right angles to the direction of propagation as shown in Fig. 1.2. The electric field is known as the optic disturbance field and is the one we are interested in when dealing with light.

Although our natural source of EMR is the sun, there are also a number of man-made sources which, among many others, include tungsten filament lamps, gas discharge lamps, and lasers. Light is that narrow band of EMR mediated by the human eye, and is limited to a spectrum extending from 380 nm to 760 nm. Other animals also see light of course, but to different extents. As we shall see later, light and colour *can* be quantified—but the human observer must always be taken into account when studying the visual sciences and photometry.

When considering the passage of light it is important to stress the medium of propagation, because in media other than space (vacuum) light will slow down—as in glass or water, for example. And if the velocity of light in a vacuum ($V_0$) is $300 \times 10^6$ ms$^{-1}$, then its velocity in a medium of refractive index ($n$) is ($V_n$) and can be found from:

$$V_n = V_0/n \qquad (1.1)$$

So, for glass of $n = 1.5$, the velocity of light travelling through that glass will be $200 \times 10^6$ ms$^{-1}$.

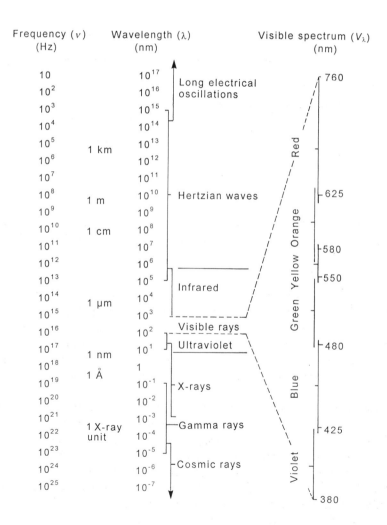

*Fig. 1.1* The spectrum of electromagnetic radiation (EMR). Units are in nanometers ($10^{-9}$m).

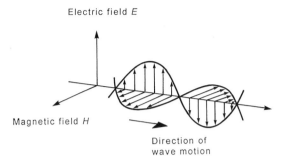

Electric field *E*

Magnetic field *H*

Direction of
wave motion

*Fig. 1.2* The electromagnetic wave.

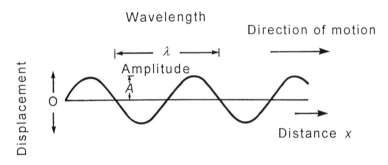

Wavelength

Direction of motion

Displacement

$\lambda$

Amplitude

O

$\hat{A}$

Distance *x*

*Fig. 1.3* A transverse electromagnetic wave of wavelength ($\lambda$) and amplitude ($A$).

Inspection of Fig. 1.3 shows that the distance between one wave crest and the next is the wavelength ($\lambda$), which has an associated frequency ($v$) directly related to *c* by the equation:

$$\lambda = c\,/\,v \qquad\qquad (1.2)$$

Commonly known as the speed of light, *c* is a universal constant, and although it is convenient to discuss optics mainly in terms of wavelengths, it is the associated frequency that is fundamentally more important since, regardless of whether light is radiated in vacuo ($V_0$) or media ($V_n$) the frequency remains invariant and only the wavelength changes (Eq: 1.2). But, apart from this, it is more convenient to discuss optical matters in terms of $\lambda$ since frequencies have such high values. An example will make this clear.

In visual optics we often refer to green light since this is the region of maximum human eye sensitivity, and if we consider green light at a wavelength of, say, 500 nanometres (500 $\times$ 10$^{-9}$ metres) it is easy to fit this value into various calculations. But if we look at the associated frequency we find (from Eq: 1.2) that $v = c\,/\,\lambda = 300 \times 10^6\,/\,500 \times 10^{-9}$, which is $6 \times 10^{14}$ Hz or, to be more emphatic, 600 000 000 000 000 cycles per second! Obviously, it is more convenient to discuss EMR in terms of wavelengths (nm) rather than frequencies (Hertz)!

The amplitude of the wave ($A$) shown in Fig.1.3 indicates the amount of light (EMR) associated with that wave, but since the human eye and sensors such as photographic film and solid-state devices are what are known as *square law detectors* all measurements of EMR are taken from the intensity of radiation $I$ where

$$I = A^2 \tag{1.3}$$

(Only in holography do we manage to record information by amplitude of the waves, and that is due to the phenomenon of optical interference.)

### *Travelling wave equation*

As shown in Fig. 1.3, the travelling wave repeats itself every wavelength unit ($\lambda$) along the x-axis of propagation, and its sine wave can be described by the function

$$\psi(x, t) = A\sin(kx - \omega t) \tag{1.4}$$

where:
   $k$ (the circular wave number) $= 2\pi/\lambda$
   $\omega$ (the circular frequency) $= 2\pi v$
   $t$ is the situation at time t

## 1.2 Coherent Sources of Light

Before we can explain *coherence* it is necessary to understand the rather chaotic nature of radiation and examine the atomic process that gives rise to the emission of light. And although we shall deal with the quantum theory of EMR at a later stage (albeit very superficially), it is worth mentioning the role of the atom at this point.

Inside the atom electrons exist in discrete energy levels, and if an electron falls from one energy level to another with lower energy, the excess energy is given off as EMR with a corresponding frequency. Under appropriate conditions therefore, the atom can be regarded as an oscillator, and when it stops vibrating those frequencies of radiation cease to be emitted. Each atom of the material emits waves of radiation during a period of about $10^{-8}$ seconds, this process being repeated again and again in a random fashion. Even if waves from different atoms all had the same frequency (as with a laser) they would always have a different phase. As a consequence a wave-train of light will only have constant phase during a period of roughly $10^{-8}$ seconds.

### *Optical coherence*

According to Fig. 1.3 and Eq: 1.4, the travelling wave looks rather simple, but in reality the frequency of the sinusoidal disturbance will vary (very slowly) and the amplitude will fluctuate too.

As we have seen, if a light source is totally coherent then each point on the source will give rise to the same type of wave, at the same instant of time, and all in phase with each other. Unfortunately this is not the case (apart from some lasers) and although it is of no great concern in photography it does provide some theoretical and practical problems with interferometric apparatus and in holography.

Optical coherence can be divided into two parts, *temporal coherence* and *spatial coherence*.

*Temporal Coherence*

The average wave-train will exist for a time period ($\Delta t_c$) which is known as the *coherence time* and is the inverse of the *frequency bandwidth* ($\Delta v$). Coherence time is also known as temporal coherence and is given as:

$$\Delta t_c = 1/\Delta v \tag{1.5}$$

Coherent waves need not be exactly in phase (where each wave emits a crest or trough simultaneously) but the phase relationship should remain fixed during the period of observation.

In holography temporal coherence is very important since it controls the *coherence length* of the wave-train ($\Delta x$) where:

$$\Delta x = c\Delta t_c \tag{1.6}$$

or, in terms of wavelength bandwidth ($\Delta \lambda$), an easier equation is:

$$\Delta x \approx \lambda^2/\Delta \lambda \tag{1.7}$$

For a typical HeNe laser emitting at $\lambda = 632.8$ nm, we can expect a bandwidth ($\Delta \lambda$) in the region of 0.002 nm (the related frequency bandwidth follows the proportional relationship: $(\Delta v/v) \propto (\Delta \lambda/\lambda)$, giving an associated frequency bandwidth $\Delta v \approx 1.5 \times 10^9$ Hz). Both Eq: 1.6 and Eq: 1.7 show that the HeNe laser can be expected to provide a coherence length ($\Delta x$) of about 20 cm, within which distance we can assume reasonable phase relationships to exist. Under these circumstances it is possible to arrange for a small object to be placed within the coherence length of a holographic optical set-up.

*Spatial coherence*

A light source that is spatially coherent offers a planar wavefront at the object. To do this, it is necessary that each point of the source acts in phase with every other point. The classical way of approaching this condition is to restrict the size of the source to point dimensions—but this can only be done at the expense of restricting the intensity of the source. However, with the advent of the laser the problem became much easier since this type of source can produce beams with very high spatial coherence, and which (in the TEM$_{oo}$ mode—an almost perfect state of laser radiation) generally have a divergence of only one minute of arc or less.

## 1.3 Geometrical Optics

Inspection of Fig. 1.3 indicates that we can think of light radiating in straight lines—in every possible direction! This is the classical theory for the propagation of light, and it is just as useful today as it was in Isaac Newton's time. Known as the rectilinear propagation of light, it is the basis of geometrical optics and is generally employed to demonstrate ray-paths for all optical instruments, including cameras, and for calculating optical relationships such as image formation and scale.

Typical examples of geometric optics are those used to show image formation by a lens, as shown in Fig. 1.4, where ray-paths for image formation with a positive lens are illustrated. The well-known 'lens equation' relates object and image conjugates ($u$) and ($v$) respectively, to the focal length of the lens ($f$) according to:

$$1/f = 1/u + 1/v \tag{1.8}$$

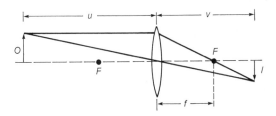

*Fig. 1.4* Image formation with a single lens. Object and image conjugates (*u* and *v*) are related to focal length (*f*) by: $1/f = 1/u + 1/v$ where the focal length is the distance from the node of emergence of that lens to point *F*.

and since the size of the image (*I*) to that of the object (*O*) is the magnification of the system, we have:

$$M = I/O \qquad (1.9)$$

Combining Eq: 1.4 with Eq: 1.5 allows us to employ two further equations of great use to photography:

$$v = f(M + 1) \qquad (1.10)$$

$$u = f(1/M + 1) \qquad (1.11)$$

## 1.4 Wave Theory of Light

The wave theory, as illustrated by Fig. 1.3, allows us to explain optical phenomena such as *diffraction* (the bending of light around an edge), *interference* (the interaction of divided wave-fronts such that they form *interference fringes*) and *polarisation* (where light rays are polarised into one particular plane, rather than every direction). The diagram shown in Fig. 1.2 is an illustration of a single *plane-polarised* wave of light.

### Diffraction

Diffraction theory is very important when considering the optical resolution of a lens system where, in the limit, the highest possible resolution is a function of the wavelength of light employed and the relative aperture of the lens (*N*), (see Box 1). Commonly known as the *f/No* of a camera lens, the relative aperture will provide an image resolution (for a theoretically perfect lens) known as the *diffraction limited resolution* (*r*) given as:

$$r = 1.22\lambda N \qquad (1.12)$$

Thus, for a lens operating at *f*/4 (*N* = 4) and with a filter limiting the bandwidth to a peak radiation of, say, 410 nm, the theoretical resolution limit (*r*) is 2000 nm, or 2 μm. This suggests that the image would resolve two points separated by 0.002 mm. It is common practice to refer to the reciprocal of *r* in terms of spatial frequency where:

$$R = 1/r \text{ (line-pairs/mm)} \qquad (1.13)$$

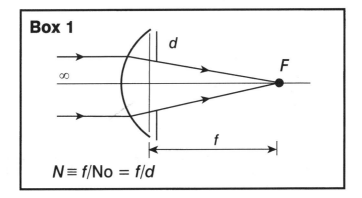

**Box 1**

$d$

$\infty$

$F$

$f$

$N \equiv f/No = f/d$

In the above example this would mean: 1/0.002 mm = 500 LP/ mm. (Note: With small apertures, such as $f$/22, resolution is degraded by the effects of diffraction, i.e., where light is bent from its normal path at the edges of small apertures.)

## *Interference*

As mentioned above, when two common wavefronts interfere they can create bright intensity fringes where the crests or troughs of individual amplitudes come together and, conversely, dark fringes where troughs meet crests. It is possible to employ an optical set-up that will exploit such conditions: holography is based upon interference phenomena, and many scientific instruments rely on either wavefront-splitting or amplitude-splitting techniques to provide for the interferometric analysis of matter.

## *Polarisation*

Natural polarisation of light can take place either by scattering or by specular reflection. With the former condition we find that blue sky is a result of preferential scattering of blue wavelengths according to Wein's law where scatter is given by:

$$\text{light scatter} \approx 1/\lambda^n \qquad (1.14)$$

where the exponent can be anything from 1 to 4 (for perfect blue skies).

But since this phenomenon is accompanied by partial polarisation, we can use a polarising filter (which reduces the transmitted light to a single plane of polarisation—and to reduced intensity of course) to exclude the scattered short wavelength light and thus darken the blue sky in colour photography. It must be noted, however, that the entire sky will not be polarised to the same degree. Scattered skylight is mainly polarised in directions at right angles to the line-of-sight of the sun.

Another use of a polarising filter is to reduce unwanted specular reflections coming from glass or water surfaces. According to 'Brewster's law' specular reflections are polarised at an angle given by:

$$\tan \theta = n \qquad (1.15)$$

(where $n = 1.333$ for water and 1.52 for crown glass).

Thus, for glass ($n = 1.52$) the angle whose tangent is 1.52 is close to 57°, as shown in Fig. 1.5.

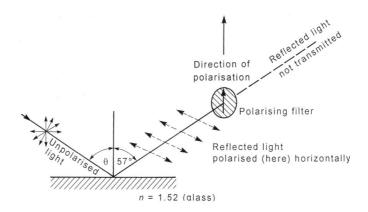

*Fig. 1.5* Specular reflections are polarised at the Brewster Angle $\theta$, where $\theta = \text{Tan}^{-1}\ n$.

# 1.5 Quantum Theory of Radiation

Although we usually think of light as a wave, when it is absorbed by matter it behaves as if it were a stream of tiny particles of energy called *photons* and which can be represented by finite wave-trains, or wave-packets. In general we talk of *photons* when discussing all forms of EMR.

In this book we make use of all three concepts of light, but the quantum theory is perhaps most useful when considering the interactive nature of EMR on sensitive materials such as the crystal structure of silver halides (AgH), and silicon sensors such as MOS (metal oxide semiconductors) or CMOS (complementary metal oxide semiconductors) as used in CCDs. In all of these materials the imaging theory is the same—a packet of EMR energy is incident upon a sensitive material, and an electron is released from the valency band of the crystal into the conduction band (see below).

## *The energy band model of an atom*

The usual model of an atom is that of a dense nucleus of positively charged *protons* surrounded by an equal number of negatively charged planetary *electrons*. This model can be used to explain the behaviour of electrons in a solid, where they are arranged within a series of concentric shells (bands) with a maximum of eight electrons per shell—in the stable state. The bands farthest from the nucleus have the greatest energy level. The outer shell is known as the *valence band*, and the number of valency electrons determines the chemical properties of the atom and also its functional relation in semiconductors. An even higher energy level is the outermost *conduction band* in which electrons can move freely in conducting an electric current.

## *The electron and electron volt*

An electron (e) has a mass of $9.109 \times 10^{-31}$ kg and a charge of $1.602 \times 10^{-19}$ coulomb (amp seconds). (One ampere = $6.24 \times 10^{18}$ electrons/second.)

The electron volt (eV) is the amount of work done when one electron is accelerated by a potential difference of one volt. One eV = $1.602 \times 10^{-19}$ joules (watt seconds).

Generally speaking, a normal atom is most stable when it has its lowest energy $E_0$, that is to say, when it is in its *ground state*, and at room temperature most of the atoms in a gas or solid occupy the ground state. In Fig. 1.6, we suppose that most of the atoms are at the ground state energy level ($E_0$) and that a single atom is in the first excited state at $E_1$. As the temperature rises more atoms will occupy a number of discrete excited states (the energy of an atom may occupy any one of the allowed higher energy levels—but not an intermediate energy value) but the population of atoms in the excited state(s) will still be much less than those at $E_0$. This is known as a *normal population* of atoms.

If the atom absorbs energy (which could be EMR in the form of a photon) and is excited to one of its allowed energy levels, say $E_1$ (from A to B in Fig. 1.6) it will emit EMR (of frequency $v$) when it falls to its ground state. The quantum of energy ($Q$) emitted is given by:

$$Q = E_1 - E_0 = hv \qquad (1.16)$$

where $h$ = Planck's constant = $6.6262 \times 10^{-34}$ Js

This is known as *spontaneous emission* of radiation, where energy is absorbed from the radiation field and re-emitted as radiation.

Fig. 1.7 represents an atom with three discrete energy levels above its stable ground state $E_0$. The first excited state is shown at $E_1$ (8 eV), the second at $E_2$ (12 eV) and the third at $E_3$ (14 eV). The atom cannot absorb incident energy that is less than the $E_1$ level, and if the atom were struck by a photon of, say, 5eV, it would not be absorbed by the atom. However, if the incident quantum is greater than 8 eV then it can be absorbed and will put the atom into its first excited state, where it will stay for a little while then fall back to the ground state, emitting its 8 eV as a packet of EMR with energy equal to $E_1 - E_0 = hv$.

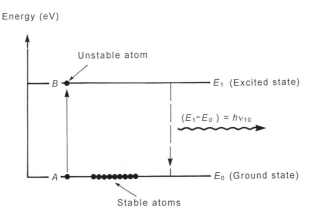

*Fig. 1.6* Simple energy level diagram. An atom excited to an allowed level $E_1$ will emit EMR of frequency $v$ when it falls to its ground state $E_0$.

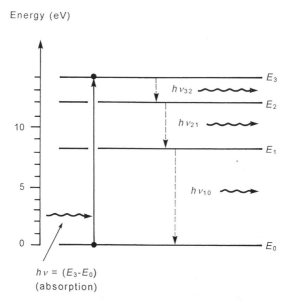

Fig. 1.7 Incoherent emission of radiation. An atom with three discrete energy levels above the stable ground state ($E_0$).

If now a photon of energy $hv = (E_3 - E_0)$ is incident on a normal population of atoms (as shown in Fig. 1.7) the probability of excitation from level $E_0$ to level $E_3$ is high since there are many more atoms in the ground state than there are in the $E_3$ level (shown here at 14 eV). As mentioned above, excited atoms eventually fall to the ground state—either directly or via intermediate states. In Fig.1.7, an atom is shown in the $E_3$ level, first falling back to $E_2$ (where it emits energy $hv_{32} = E_3 - E_2$), then makes further transitions from $E_2$ to $E_1$, and $E_1$ to $E_0$, with emissions $hv_{21}$ and $hv_{10}$ respectively.

Under these circumstances, the three spontaneous emissions depicted in Fig. 1.7 will not only have different amplitudes and frequencies but, since they occur at slightly different times, will result in totally incoherent wave-trains. If an atom in its ground state absorbs sufficient energy just to remove an electron completely from the atom, then the absorbed energy is known as the *ionisation energy*.

## Photon energy

From Eq: 1.16 we saw that a photon of light will have the energy $Q = hv$. As an example we can take an incident photon of $\lambda = 500$ nm, and from Eq: 1.2 find a value for the frequency, where $v = c/\lambda$, or $300 \times 10^6$ m s$^{-1}$/5 $\times 10^{-7} = 6 \times 10^{14}$ Hz.

The energy $Q = (6.6262 \times 10^{-34}$ J s$) (6 \times 10^{14}$ Hz$) = 39.76 \times 10^{-20}$ J, and since 1 eV is equal to $1.602 \times 10^{-19}$ J, the energy ($Q$) is 2.48 eV.

## Spectral power distribution

The spectral power distribution of a source is quoted as the number of watts radiated over some wavelength interval, for example over a specific spectral bandwidth ($\Delta\lambda$).

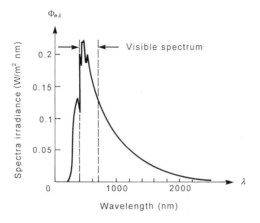

*Fig. 1.8* Spectral power distribution of the sun.

If, for example, we look at a bandwidth of 400 nm to 410 nm, the radiated power within this 10 nm bandwidth can be specified. But the amount of radiation falling at exactly 400 nm is meaningless. It is possible to choose any size of bandwidth—but the interval must be specified!

The solar spectral power distribution is shown in Fig.1.8, with the ordinate scaled in units of watts per square metre per nanometre, that is to say, the amount of spectral radiant power ($\Phi_{e\lambda}$) that falls on a square metre of the earth. If the total spectral radiant power under the curve shown in Fig. 1.8 is summed then we have the total solar radiant power per unit area as shown by the integral:

$$\Phi_e = \int_0^\infty \Phi_{e\lambda} d\lambda \quad \text{watts} \tag{1.17}$$

The total radiant power per unit area falling on the earth's upper atmosphere is known to be 1400 watts per square metre, with the amount falling on the earth's surface reduced to about 1 kW m$^{-2}$ on a clear day. The associated energy is given by:

$$Q = \Phi_e t \text{ joules} \tag{1.18}$$

where $t$ = time of exposure in seconds.

# 2 Photometry and Visual Science

## 2.1 Basic Photometry

As the name suggests, photometry is the science of measuring light, that is to say, measuring EMR within the visual limits of 380 nm to 760 nm as shown in Fig. 1.1. Whereas radiometry is pure physics, photometry is concerned with psychophysics— where the eye mediates between EMR and the brain. As a consequence we find that our observations, being totally subjective, are less accurate than those in radiometry —simply because we must take the average human observer into the equation!

Photometry accepts only a small band of the EMR ($\Delta\lambda = 380$ nm) and in many ways seems to be at odds with the more accurate system—radiometry! But photometry was already well developed before much was known about EMR and to this day we still have photometric units that reflect its historical past, that is, the unit for luminous intensity (the candela) was originally a 'standard candle' burning a specific amount of wax per hour! Nevertheless, for those dealing with visual optics alone (ophthalmics, lenses, instruments and most of photography) photometry still serves a useful purpose. But for technical and scientific purposes photography is a highly useful tool and can 'see' further than the visual limits. Film is capable of recording high-frequency radiation such as X-rays and gamma rays, as well as the near ultra-violet (including a narrow band around 320 nm using quartz optics); and is capable of recording in the near infrared up to about 1200 nm with special plates. Similarly, CCD imagery can be used outside the visible spectrum, MOS sensors being sensitive up to about 1100 nm.

### *Photometric radiation equivalent*

The unit of luminous intensity (I) is the candela (cd) which, by definition, is 1/60th of a square centimetre of the surface of a black-body radiator at the absolute temperature of 2045 K. (Note: A black-body radiator is one that absorbs all the radiation incident upon it and has no reflecting power. The radiation from a heated black-body source is called black-body radiation, and is always quoted in Kelvin—the SI unit of thermodynamic temperature. Zero degrees Kelvin is equal to –273.16°C, i.e. *absolute zero.*)

From this specification and a knowledge of the sensitivity of the human eye ($V\lambda$) it is possible to quantify the physical radiant unit into photometric terms. The human

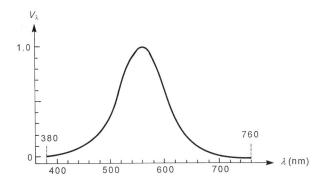

*Fig. 2.1* The $V_\lambda$ curve. Human eye sensitivity to daylight (photopic vision) shown against wavelength ($\lambda$).

eye sensitivity for daylight (*photopic* sensitivity) is shown against wavelength in Fig. 2.1, and is known as the $V_\lambda$ curve.

The photometric radiation equivalent (PRE) for monochromatic radiation is given by:

$$K_\lambda = \Phi_{v\lambda}/\Phi_{e\lambda} \tag{2.1}$$

The maximum value for $K_\lambda$ is:

$$K_{\lambda(max)} = 673 \text{ lumen/watt} \tag{2.2}$$

and this parameter allows us to find the PRE from:

$$K_\lambda = V_\lambda K_{\lambda(max)} \tag{2.3}$$

From inspection of the $V_\lambda$ curve we can see that at a wavelength of 510 nm the value is 0.503, and from Eq: 2.3 we can calculate:

$$K_\lambda = 0.503 \times 673 = 338 \text{ lumen/watt}$$

The reciprocal value of $K_{\lambda(max)}$ is known as the *mechanical equivalent of light* ($M$):

$$M = 1/K_{\lambda(max)} = 1/(673 \text{ lmW}^{-1}) = 1.47 \text{ mW/lm}$$

## Luminous flux

The amount of light energy flowing from a source is known as the *luminous flux*, and is defined as:

$$\Phi_V = K_{\lambda(max)} \int_{380 \text{ nm}}^{760 \text{ nm}} \Phi_{e\lambda} V_\lambda d\lambda \text{ (lumens)} \tag{2.4}$$

and in a given period of time ($t$) the *luminous energy* (exposure) is given by:

$$Q_V = \Phi_V t = 673t \int_{380 \text{ nm}}^{760 \text{ nm}} \Phi_{e\lambda} V_\lambda d\lambda \text{ (lm/s)} \tag{2.5}$$

## Luminous intensity

By definition, the luminous intensity ($I$) of a source is given by:

$$I = \Phi_v / d\omega \qquad (2.6)$$

where $d\omega$ is the elementary solid angle into which the source emits a flux of $d\Phi_v$.

For a luminous flux radiating into a perfect sphere of $4\pi$ steradian, a source of 1 candela provides a flux of $4\pi$ lumens:

$$\Phi_v = I \int_0^{4\pi} dw = 4\pi I \qquad (2.7)$$

So, for 1 candela of luminous intensity we get a theoretical total of 12.56 lumens.

## Illuminance

If a flux ($\Phi_v$) is incident upon a surface of area $S$ (usually $S$ is given in square metres) it is said to be *illuminated,* and the illuminance ($E$) at any point on that surface is given by:

$$E = \Phi_v / S \qquad (2.8)$$

If $S$ is quoted in square metres (m²) then $E$ is given in lumen/m², or lux.

$$E = 673 \int_{380\ nm}^{760\ nm} \Phi_{e\lambda} V_\lambda d\lambda \quad (\text{lm/m}^2) \quad (\text{lux}) \qquad (2.9)$$

## Inverse square law

The law of inverse squares is well known in photography and is the basis of the *f*/no sequence found on all camera lenses, and by which we can allow twice as much, or half as much, light to reach the film or CCD—simply by adjusting the *f*/nos, up or down, as they run in the geometric progression of √2 (i.e. *f*/2, *f*/2.8, *f*/4, *f*/5.6, *f*/8...).

The law is illustrated in Fig. 2.2, which shows a source of 20 Cd illuminating a 1 metre square card (*a*) at a distance of 1metre from the source.

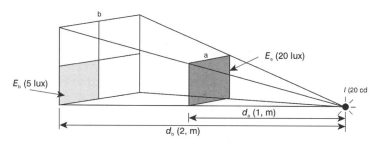

*Fig. 2.2* The law of inverse squares: The illumination of a surface falls off inversely as square of the distance from the source.

The illuminance of a surface is given by:

$$E = I/d^2 \text{ (lux)} \qquad (2.10)$$

and for surface (*a*) in Fig. 2.2, we have $E_a = 20 \text{ Cd}/1^2 = 20$ lux.

If we now want to calculate the illuminance on a second surface, such as (*b*), when we only know the value of $E_a$, then we may use:

$$E_b/E_a = (d_a/d_b)^2 \qquad (2.11)$$

Substituting, we now have:

$$E_b = E_a(d_a/d_b)^2 = 20 (1/2)^2 = 5 \text{ lux.}$$

## *Reflectance*

Reflectance ($\rho$) may take the form of *specular reflectance*, as shown in Fig. 2.3a or as *diffuse reflectance* shown in Fig. 2.3b. Specular reflectance is that exhibited by a mirror and follows a regular law where the angle of incidence (*i*) is equal to the angle of reflectance (*t*). But in photography we are more concerned with the light that is reflected from objects—and although some of the light will undoubtedly be specular (from shiny surfaces) most of it will be diffuse, and follow an irregular distribution known as an *indicatrix* of reflection with a unique form like that shown in Fig. 2.3b. The indicatrix not only illustrates the different directions of reflected light, but (by their vectors) their strengths also, and serves to describe the nature of the reflecting surface.

(a) Spectral reflectance

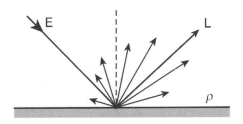

(b) Diffuse reflectance

*Fig. 2.3* (a) Specular reflection. (b) Diffuse reflection.

## *Luminance*

Although we see *by* light, we cannot actually *see* light itself! What we *do* see are the various luminances coming from an object and it is these that we interpret through eye and brain. Each luminance ($L$) can be calculated (in units of Cd/m²) as:

$$L = E\rho/\pi \,(\text{Cdm}^{-2}) \qquad (2.12)$$

For an object ($O$) with an even and diffusely reflecting surface ($\rho$), the luminance from that surface will follow Eq: 2.12, which in terms of incident flux is given by:

$$L = \frac{673}{\text{m}^2} \int_{380\,\text{nm}}^{760\,\text{nm}} \Phi_{e\lambda} V_\lambda \rho_\lambda d\lambda \qquad (2.13)$$

## 2.2 Camera Image Photometry

For a camera, the image photometry is illustrated in Fig. 2.4, where a camera lens of relative aperture ($N$) = $f/d$, is exposed via a spectral filter ($F$) of bandwidth $F_\lambda$. Under these circumstances we can say that the spectrally defined luminance of the object is now:

$$L_{o\lambda} = \frac{673}{\text{m}^2} \int_{380\,\text{nm}}^{760\,\text{nm}} \Phi_{e\lambda} F_\lambda V_\lambda \rho_\lambda d\lambda \quad (\text{Cdm}^{-2}) \qquad (2.14)$$

## *Image illuminance*

In simple terms image illuminance ($E_i$) is only a function of object luminance and camera aperture, as shown:

$$E_i = L_o/N^2 \,(\text{lux}) \qquad (2.15)$$

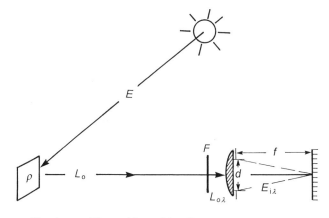

*Fig. 2.4* From an illuminance ($E$), an object with reflectance ($\rho$) presents a luminance ($L_o$) incident on the filter ($F$). The camera lens receives a spectral luminance ($L_{o\lambda}$) through the relative aperture ($N = f/d$), to provide an image illuminance $E_{i\lambda}$.

and if a filter is employed then the spectrally limited (monochrome) image illuminance is given by:

$$E_{i\lambda} = L_{o\lambda}/N^2 \text{ (lux)} \qquad (2.16)$$

Note: The lens aperture ($N$) is squared because of the law of inverse squares which is responsible for the $f$/no progression and the common acceptance that camera exposure is controlled by factors of 2, that is, it is the area of the lens aperture that doubles when the diameter goes up by $\sqrt{2}$ (one stop): area $\propto$ diameter$^2$.

Unfortunately camera image illuminance is complicated by three additional factors:

- *lens transmission ($T_g$),*
- *off-axis image illumination,*
- *non-image light (lens flare).*

## Lens transmission

Lens transmission is never 100%, but suffers from internal reflections at each air/glass interface. The degree of attenuation can be normalised for most compound lenses, with $m$ air/glass surfaces, and is given by:

$$T_g = (0.98)^m \qquad (2.17)$$

Typically, for an uncoated compound lens with six air/glass surfaces, $T_g = 0.88$.

## Off-axis image illuminance

The angle ($\theta$) made between the optical axis and extreme off-axis image points gives rise to less image illuminance ($E_{i\theta}$) at those points, and should be accounted for when considering an average level of image illuminance. If we look at a mid-field image point that lies at an off-axis angle ($\theta$), we can allow for this problem by calculating the off-axis illuminance as a fraction of the axial illuminance $E_i$.

$$E_{i\theta} = E_i \cos \theta^4 \qquad (2.18)$$

Thus, for off-axis points lying 25° from the axis, the image illuminance at these points will be reduced to $0.67E_i$. Taking the above values for $T_g$ and $E_{i\theta}$ into account, we can modify Eq: 2.15 and 2.16 by including the factor ($k$), where $k$ is the product of the two values, that is $0.67 \times 0.88 = 0.59$. The general equation for monochromatic spectral image illuminance is therefore:

$$E_{i\lambda} = k L_{o\lambda}/N^2 \text{ (lux)} \qquad (2.19)$$

and specifically, for the parameters calculated for $k$ (above), we can put:

$$E_{il} = 0.59 L_{o\lambda}/N^2 \text{ (lux)} \qquad (2.20)$$

## Lens flare

In all optical instruments there is an amount of non-image light present, usually known as lens flare ($E_{if}$). Most of this 'flare-light' is caused by the internal reflections mentioned above, but in addition there are possible reflections from the inner walls of the lens barrel and, in the case of CCD images, the influence of the MOS sensors themselves—including cell filters, chip thickness and also the direction of the image illuminance (front or back lit illuminance).

As a consequence the total image illuminance ($E_{iT}$) is given by:

$$E_{iT} = E_i + E_{if} \text{ (lux)} \tag{2.21}$$

Generally speaking the value of $E_{if}$ is rarely known with any degree of accuracy, nevertheless it is always present. But with cameras that are of good quality and in fresh condition flare-light can usually be ignored.

### Camera exposure

For the general case it only requires the exposure time ($t$) to be included and we have the equation for camera exposure:

$$H_i = (0.59 \, L_o/N^2) \, t \ \text{ (lux seconds)} \tag{2.22}$$

If a filter is included in the system, as shown in Fig. 2.4, then the luminance should be that indicated in Eq: 2.20.

## 2.3 The Visual System

### Brightness

Brightness ($B$) is the subjective correlate of luminance and its relationship to luminance is a highly complex function depending upon the adaptive state of the eye, inhibitory factors (such as the influence of adjacent image areas) and lightness and colour constancies. [1] Brightness is a function of both achromatic (black and white) and colour scenes and its values can only be determined approximately by means of psychological scaling procedures. It is perhaps strange that the most obvious feature of imagery—the varying degrees of brightness we perceive when viewing the image of a scene—is the least understood part of the entire reproduction cycle. Regardless of the medium, silver or silicon, the final result still has to be interpreted through the vagaries of the human visual system.

For simple fields (such as a single luminance prominent within a uniform background) Stevens and Stevens[2] have shown that the magnitude of the brightness sensation can be determined by direct estimation and by judging brightness ratios. The variability of each observer and the variations due to personal interpretation all contribute to brightness being a statistical quantity with a basic uncertainty. Nevertheless, according to a number of authorities [3, 4, 5] the power law which satisfies the basic relationship for simple fields is:

$$B = kL_o{}^n \tag{2.23}$$

where:

$B$ is the psychological magnitude of brightness,

$L_o$ is the luminance of a scene element observed within a simple field,

$n$ is the exponent for brightness, generally agreed to be of the order of 0.33 for simple fields,

$k$ is a constant which depends upon the conditions of the test.

In complex (everyday) scenes, certain modifications are needed to basic brightness scales, because of adaptation, induction and lightness constancy. As an example of the complexity involved in this subject the reader is invited to inspect Fig. 2.5, where an everyday example of lightness constancy has been recorded in a photograph. The panel fixed to the wall above the table is evenly illuminated to match the luminance of the panel fixed below the table. The upper panel has a reflectance ($\rho$) of 0.18, whereas the panel below the table has a reflectance of 0.84. Although the illuminance ($E$) has been adjusted to provide conditions of equal luminance ($L$) between the two panels there is no doubt that the lower panel looks 'lighter' than the one above. A 1 : 1 relationship exists between the print and the scene, with respect to the panels, and it can be shown that they both have identical reflection densities[1] (see Box 2). But if a mask is placed over the photograph, obscuring all but the two panels, then it will be seen that they exhibit identical brightness—thus illustrating the well-known fact that at least two different surfaces must be in view at the same time in order to gain *lightness constancy*.

From this single example of the problems associated with brightness in the visual scene, it is evident that brightness in complex fields cannot be estimated with an expression as simple as that shown in Eq: 2.23.

Through research investigating complex field brightnesses in interior scenes Graham[6] has shown that an empirical expression, in the form of a polynominal, gave good results over three levels of illuminance. The second term in Eq: 2.24 may be considered as the departure from the simple power law that is to be expected for an expression concerned with a complex field.

$$B_0 = aL_0^b + \text{antilog } c(\log_{10} L_0)^n \qquad (2.24)$$

*Fig. 2.5* An example of lightness constancy. Although the luminance is the same for both grey patches, the upper patch ($\rho = 0.18$) still *looks* darker than the one below ($\rho = 0.84$).

---

**Box 2**

If I is the light incident upon a surface of reflectance ($\rho$), then the opacity of the surface ($O$) is given by $O = I/\rho$. Since $I$ can be considered as unity, we have $O = 1/\rho$. For example, for $\rho = 0.5$ the opacity is 2. Similarly, for a semi-transparent medium we can put $O = 1/T$ (a photographic negative has numerous transparencies ($T$) in its image). Density ($D$) is given as $D = \log_{10} 1/T$ or $1/\rho$.

---

where:

$n$ is the logarithm of the scene luminance range (for $E_0 = 640$ lux, $n = 1.862$), and the constants

$a$, $b$ and $c$ are found by iteration to be 1.025, 1.53 and –0.32 respectively.
Fitting the above values into Eq: 2.24 gives the empirical equation:

$$B_0 = 1.025L_0^{1.53} / \text{antilog } 0.32(\log_{10}L_0)^{1.862} \qquad (2.25)$$

The plot of Eq: 2.25, showing log of brightness ($B$) against log of scene luminance ($L_0$) is shown in Fig. 2.6. It can be seen that Eq: 2.25 provides a good fit for the three adaptation levels of 40, 174 and 640 lux.

## *Monochrome tone reproduction with photographic film*

In an attempt to reproduce an exact monochrome likeness to original scene interiors Graham[1, 6] selected materials and processes with specific controls to gain optimal results. With the aid of an eight block cascade of tone reproduction diagrams (Fig. 2.7) it was possible to show an almost perfect result for restricted conditions.

*Fig. 2.6* Logarithm of relative scene brightness ($B$) plotted against scene luminance ($L_0$) at three adaptation levels.

Although such monochrome reproductions were proven possible, the system was difficult and time consuming.

Inspection of Fig. 2.7 shows the reproduction cycle as it reads from Block 1, going clockwise to the final Block 8. It is instructive to note the laborious cycle of reproduction, as set out in Table. 2.1.

Table 2.1 *(see also Fig. 2.7)*

| | |
|---|---|
| Block 1. | Log scene luminance ($L_o$) v log scene brightness ($B_o$). |
| Block 2. | Camera lens flare (non-linear in shadow areas of image reproduction). |
| Block 3. | Kodak Plus-X film: density v log exposure (typically non-linear, as are all films). |
| Block 4. | Enlarger flare (almost linear in this instance). |
| Block 5. | Bromide paper density v log exposure scale (typically sigmoid in shape). |
| Block 6. | Print viewing: log print luminance v log print density (linear). |
| Block 7. | Log print luminance ($L_p$) v log print brightness ($B_p$). |
| Block 8. | Overall tone reproduction (almost linear). |

Table 2.1 serves to illustrate the extended process of photography, from camera through film, enlarging and printing. Although a very reasonable monochrome facsimile *can* be gained, it is obvious that the process is far from straightforward—mainly due to the non-linearity of photographic films and papers. Leaving aside the purely subjective issues involved, the simple relationship between scene luminance ($L_o$) and print density ($D_p$) indicates a non-linear objective tone reproduction, as shown in Fig. 2.8.

### *Monochrome tone reproduction with digital cameras*

It has long been recognised that CCD imagers provide a linear response to scene luminances, and there can be little doubt that this also extends to colour reproduction. Naturally a 1 : 1 response between scene and image must also depend upon the camera optics (digital sensor arrays are not always free from flare) and the computer printout, but from a simple experiment carried out by me it appears that a 1 : 1 response can be assumed for even modest digital cameras.

Using the Kodak DC-40 digital camera with a 3 diopter close-up lens attachment, a monochrome grey scale was recorded and its image downloaded into Kodak PhotoEnhancer software. The resulting computer image was then printed out on an inkjet printer to yield a facsimile grey scale. The original and facsimile grey-scale densities are shown in Table. 2.2, and plotted to show the linear 1 : 1 response shown in Fig. 2.9.

Obviously the linear response of CCDs will prove to be a significant advantage in the development of digital camera applications.

## 2.4 Colour

The physical nature of colour was first understood by Isaac Newton (1642–1727), who used a glass prism to display a colour spectrum from incident white light, as

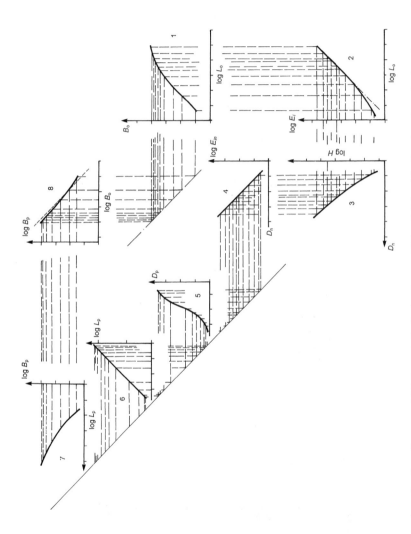

*Fig. 2.7* Overall tone reproduction diagram which is read clockwise from middle of right side. Starting from the interior scene brightness function (1), camera lens curve (2), Plus-X film (3), enlarger curve (4), printing paper curve (5), print-viewing conditions (6), print brightness function (7) and final tone-reproduction curve (8).

WSG.1.S Bromide paper
processed in D.19 (1:2)
20°C, 80 seconds

*Fig. 2.8* Experimental plot of log print density $D_p$ against log scene luminance $L_o$. Recorded on Kodak Plus-X film type 4147 via Wratten 8 filter. Processed in Kodak Microdol-X, 12 minutes at 20°C.

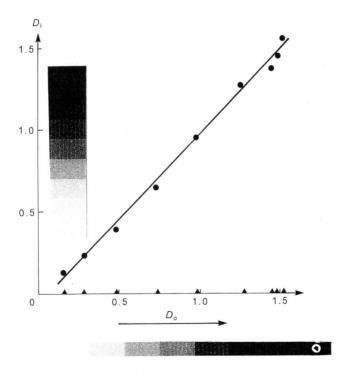

*Fig. 2.9* Typical CCD linear response between original and facsimile grey-scale densities: Kodak DC-40 camera.

| Table 2.2 | |
| --- | --- |
| Original grey-scale densities | Printed grey-scale densities from Kodak DC-40 camera |
| $D_o$ | $D_i$ |
| 0.16 | 0.12 |
| 0.29 | 0.24 |
| 0.49 | 0.38 |
| 0.73 | 0.65 |
| 0.99 | 0.95 |
| 1.27 | 1.26 |
| 1.44 | 1.37 |
| 1.48 | 1.45 |
| 1.52 | 1.55 |

shown in Fig. 2.10 (see colour section). Newton also realised that colour is a *perception*: it needs someone to receive the rays of light in order to interpret them as colour. He made this quite clear in a passage from his major work *OPTIKS*: 'For the rays, to speak properly, are not coloured. In them there is nothing else than a certain power and disposition to stir up a sensation of this or that colour.'

If a material should absorb white light evenly throughout the spectrum, then it will appear neutral; as a shade of grey, or (if absorption is almost complete) as black. But most materials absorb only parts of the visible spectrum and reflect the rest. This selective absorption gives rise to the sensation of colour—we see the light that is not absorbed.

Colour is an entirely subjective phenomenon and relies on special nerve cells, called cones, in the retina of the eye. Three different types of cone exist, each being responsible for the detection of a different part of the visible spectrum: one to red light, one to green and one to blue light. The three types of cone are arranged in a random mosaic in the fovea of the retina. If red light falls on the retina, essentially only the red sensitive cones send signals to the brain, and we perceive this radiation as the colour red.

It was Thomas Young (1773–1829) who first discovered that the eye perceives colours as a mixture of only three different *primary colours*. His famous demonstration is illustrated in Fig. 2.11a (see colour section). Three projectors are arranged so that overlapping circles of red, green and blue light are projected onto a screen. At each overlap the coloured lights add to produce different colours. In the centre, all three colours add to give white light. This is called the *additive synthesis of colour*. These three primary colours (red, green, blue) are fundamental to our understanding of colour vision, but more important they are, with their complementary colours (cyan, magenta and yellow—formed by overlapping primary colours of light), basic to colour imagery, both photographic and digital.

Just as the *additive* (spectral) *primaries* add to form white, so we can use their complementaries, cyan, magenta and yellow, to subtract colour. If, instead of using beams of coloured light, we start with a white screen and add coloured filters to it, a different effect is obtained. This is because the white screen already reflects white light containing all three additive primary colours. Adding coloured filters *subtracts* portions of the spectrum. If we take, say, a yellow filter and hold it in front of a white screen, then the yellow absorbs the blue light and reflects a mixture of red and green light, which appears yellow to the eye, so we see a yellow screen. If we now put a cyan filter over the yellow, then we see green. Finally, if we put cyan, magenta and yellow filters together all three additive primary colours have been absorbed (subtracted from white) so we get black. For this reason the complementary colours are known as *subtractive primaries*. This type of colour synthesis is shown in Fig. 2.11b.

Summing up we can put:

**Additive primary colours**
Red + Green + Blue = White

| **Additive primaries** | **Complementary colours** |
|---|---|
| Red + Green | Yellow |
| Red + Blue | Magenta |
| Green + Blue | Cyan |

**Subtractive primaries**
Cyan + Magenta + Yellow = Black

A convenient way of remembering these relationships is to use the simple matrix given below:

**R  G  B**

**C  M  Y**

Each complementary colour is made up of the two additive primaries not directly above, for example: C = G + B. And each of the additive primaries can be seen by combining the two complementary colours not directly below. Obviously there are more than just six colours—in fact if we take differences in brightness and purity (restricted bandwidth) into account then we can distinguish millions of discrete colours, but only a few hundreds at any one time!

To be correct we should discuss 'colour' in terms of *hue*, *saturation* and *lightness*, where 'lightness' is the term used instead of 'brightness'. Two major systems for depicting colour are the Munsell system and the CIE system.

## *Munsell colour system*

The Munsell system is shown schematically in Fig. 2.12. It is a practical system and as such is built as a three-dimensional model known as a Munsell tree (or colour solid), or can be purchased as a book. Essentially the Munsell system of colour notation identifies colour in terms of three attributes: hue, value (lightness) and chroma (saturation).

## Hue

This is simply the name we give to a colour (red, yellow, etc.), and in the Munsell system these are represented around a three-dimensional colour tree, with forty leaves of constant hue.

## Saturation (chroma)

Saturation is the purity of a colour. Most colours have some grey in them (they are not pure) but if a colour has no grey in it it is said to be fully saturated. The 'leaf' of constant hue shows increasing saturation as the colour squares shift to the edge of the leaf.

## Lightness (value)

Lightness is simply a scale going from black (1) at the bottom of the tree, to white (10) at the top. The complete Munsell notation for a colour is written as: HV/C. Thus, for a 'rose' colour its notation might be 5R 6/4.

## CIE colour system

The CIE (Commission Internationale de l'Éclairage) system takes the form of strongly modified colour triangle and also takes into account the source of illumination when specifying the colour under investigation. It is a scientific system which allows the user to plot the colour characteristics of a filter or paint or whatever, at some point within the locus of the CIE diagram. The locus of the diagram starts at 700 nm at the bottom right-hand edge of the figure and extends through green at 520 nm down to 400 nm (blue) at the lower left. The straight line connecting the blue and red ends represents the non-spectral colours of magenta (i.e. complementary to green opposite).

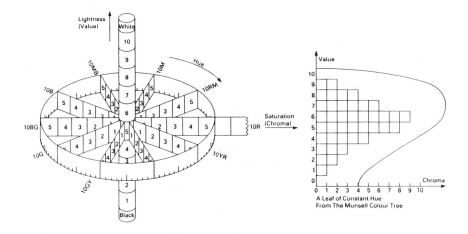

*Fig. 2.12* The Munsell colour system.

As shown in Fig. 2.13, the CIE diagram also places the light source within the figure. In the example shown, three well-known illuminants *A*, *B* and *C* are provided. However, if the *x*, *y* coordinates of any other light source are known then it too can be positioned within the locus. In Fig. 2.13 the *x*, *y* coordinates for a Kodak Wratten 58 filter are plotted for light sources *A* and *C*. Kodak provide full information on their filters and for the illuminant *A* (high wattage tungsten lamp at 2854 K) the standard green 58 filter has coordinates $x_A = 0.269$, $y_A = 0.683$ and a total visual transmission of 16.9%. For the *C* type illuminant (sunlight plus skylight at 6500 K) the *x*, *y* coordinates are 0.242 and 0.692, with visual transmission at 12.5%.

The location of these two coordinates are shown in Fig. 2.13, and if a line is extended from the light source through the appropriate coordinate point then it will cut the locus at the dominant wavelength transmitted by the green filter when used under that illuminant. In this instance the dominant wavelengths are 539.5 nm for the *A* source and 541.2 nm for the *C* source.

The saturated colours lie along the locus and become less saturated as the coordinates move towards the centre of the figure. Lightness is not available directly since this is only a two-dimensional representation of a colour. To find the complementary colour of the dominant wavelength the line that cuts the locus need only be extended backwards. For the greens this backward extension reaches the non-spectral magenta line.

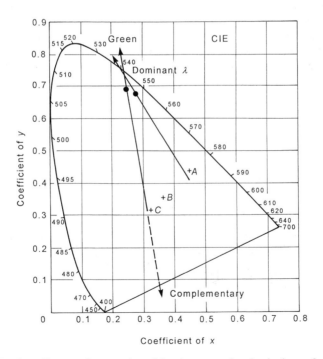

*Fig. 2.13* CIE colour diagram. Construction of dominant wavelenghts is shown for the Wratten 58 green filter (coordinates within the locus of the diagram), and light sources A and C.

## Photographic colour films and papers

All modern colour films (except Polarcolor) and papers are based on the subtractive principles of colour reproduction and consist of multi-layered emulsions with complementary dyes coupled to the oxidation products of silver halide development. The greater the amount of silver image, the greater the amount of dye. Thus, for negative colour film, a scene colour of say, yellow, will affect the red and green sensitive layers of the tri-pack and these, in turn, will produce cyan and magenta dyes. The resulting negative colour will be a combination of the cyan and magenta dyes – giving blue! When printed, a similar type of tri-pack emulsion will receive blue light in its blue sensitive layer—which then couples to the original scene colour of yellow.

## Digital colour images

For digital colour both additive and subtractive principles are involved. The pixel array camera has an array of many thousands of small picture elements (pixels), each of the order of about 10 μm as a rule. These pixels are covered with individual filters, such that red, green and blue sensors are always adjacent. When this additive colour array is downloaded to the computer (via an analogue to digital converter) the information is compiled as an additive colour system and what we see on the monitor is an image made up from RGB phosphors. But when the image is transported to the colour printer the data are then converted to CMYK for either inkjet, laser or dye-sublimation printing with cyan, magenta, yellow and black inks. The black (K) is added to give printing strength to the image, for although in theory cyan, magenta and yellow inks combine to give black, in practice they rarely do so because of ink imperfections.

Whereas in theory a colour photograph could have an infinite number of colours, in digital imagery colour is restricted to what is known as *colour depth.* Colour depth is expressed in terms of the amount of computer memory allocated to defining the colours for each pixel. An 8 bit colour, for example, gives a palette of $2^8$ or 256 colours per pixel, a 16 bit gives 65 536, and a 24 bit gives 16.7 million.

Although we have mentioned the pixel array camera, this is not the only way of producing colour in digital cameras and, as we shall see later, there are special cameras that take three simultaneous or consecutive exposures through separate red, green and blue filters. The advantage of these systems is that the original pixel resolution is not reduced to account for the filters. But these cameras are really only suitable for stationary subjects and limited to studio use.

# 3   Fundamentals of Imaging Systems

## 3.1  Types of Imaging Systems

According to Klein[7] and Metz, Ruchti and Seidel,[8] imaging systems can be classified into four basic types according to the character (stochastic or multilevel), and to the spatial arrangement (regular or random) of the constituent image elements.

### *Regular/stochastic*

The regular arrangement of newsprint images (such as letterpress) employs only black dots on a white ground to enable the appearance of whites, greys and blacks. When viewed under normal observation the eye confuses these dots (image elements) to yield a picture that appears as one of continuous tone. But under moderate magnification the dot structure is revealed and it can be seen that, although regular in spatial distribution, dot size governs image density. In such a system the stochastic (statistical) nature of the image is one of binary elements (on-off detectors) that can only assume extremes of a given density range, for example, black (1) or white (0). Any grey tone between black and white being achieved only within an area considerably larger than a single element, and with a suitable statistical mix of black and white elements.

### *Random/stochastic*

If we make an image with a very high-contrast high-resolution film, we can expect the image structure to be a random collection of black image points, each with a point spread function (PSF) of about 1.0 μm diameter at the 10% intensity level. When scanned by an aperture much larger than the PSF (such as the human eye, or a micro-densitometer) we would interpret a large number of such dots as a continuous black area. But if only half this number occupied the same area, then the impression would be a grey, and so on down to white—where perhaps only a single dot (PSF) occupies the scanned area. A typical PSF for Kodak Plus-X film is shown in Fig. 3.1, where the 10% level is 26 μm diameter. It can be seen that with either regular or random arrangements, both of the stochastic systems rely on statistical distributions of black and white image elements (dots or PSFs).

### *Random/multilevel*

Whereas high-contrast films have a random distribution of small, almost equally sized grains of AgH, conventional panchromatic films also have a size distribution which

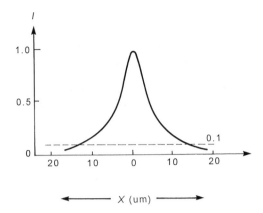

*Fig. 3.1* Point spread function (PSF).

allows for a wide range of density levels. As a result, there is a greater latitude for accepting various scene luminances in a single exposure. We can therefore say that conventional photography is of the random/multilevel type of imaging system. A typical sample of grains taken from a fast panchromatic film is shown in Fig. 3.2, where the grain-size distribution ranges from about 0.5 μm to 3 μm diameter. The 'printed-out' specks shown within individual grains in Fig. 3.2, are microdensities due to microscope illumination and not to any development.

From such a system the developed image can be expected to have multilevels of density (*M*) given by:

$$M = (\Delta D/2kG_S)A^{0.5} + 1 \tag{3.1}$$

where:

$\Delta D$ is the density range in the image,
$G_s$ is the Selwyn granularity averaged over $\Delta D$,

*Fig. 3.2* Typical silver halide grains taken from a fast panchromatic film. Grain size distribution ranges from 0.5 mm to 3 mm.

$k$ is the number of standard deviations ($\sigma$) by which adjacent density levels are separated; for a normal distribution of densities $k$ is $\pm5\sigma_D$, but intervals of $10\sigma_D$ are recommended to avoid abnormal distributions of density readings,

$A$ is the area of scanning aperture (cell size).

Film granularity (system noise) is usually given in terms of $G_S$ (quoted above) and is the statistical variation of microdensities (usually found for an image density of 1.0) that can be expected for a given film material. Selwyn granularity is calculated as:

$$G_S = \sigma_D A^{0.5} \text{ (density microns)} \qquad (3.2)$$

where $\sigma_D$ is the root mean square (RMS) granularity value (statistically the standard deviation $\sigma$) taken from multiple microdensitometer readings and calculated according to Eq: 3.3.

$$\sigma_D = ((\Sigma(\Delta D)^2)/(n-1))^{0.5} \qquad (3.3)$$

Kodak Ltd use an aperture of 48 µm diameter for its quoted RMS granularity values,[9] which are simplified to the form of:

$$G_{RMS} = 10^3\sigma_D \qquad (3.4)$$

As an example, we could calculate the density levels ($M$) for Kodak Plus-X film with the following parameters: $G_S = 0.8$, $\Delta D = 1.4$, $k = 10$, and $A = 530$ square microns (an area provided by the diameter of a typical Plus-X, PSF at the 10% level). From Eq: 3.1, we have:

$$M = ((1.4/20 \times 0.8) \times (530)^{0.5}) + 1 = ((0.0875) \times (23)) + 1 \approx 3$$

So we can say that, for Plus-X film under the above conditions, we can expect three separate density levels in a single PSF. We shall see later that $M$ is important when calculating the information capacity of an imaging system.

### *Regular/multilevel*

Regular/multilevel imaging systems include CCD imagers, where we have a regular array of pixels each with a multilevel capacity ($M$) of grey tones or colour. When CCD type imagers were first put on the market they were very coarse with arrays of the order of only 400 × 400 pixels. Nevertheless, by the mid-1970s CCD cameras were being used in astronomy; in the 1990s we have cameras with multi-million pixel arrays available for conventional camera work. For CCD imaging systems with their multilevel character and regular arrangement of elements (pixels) the information capacity ($I_c$) can be determined very easily.

## 3.2 Information Capacity

According to Shannon[10] information capacity ($I_c$) is defined as the maximum amount of information a system is capable of storing under optimum conditions of encoding. For a multilevel system comprising $n$ elements, with $M$ levels each, the capacity (in binary digits, or bits) is given by:

$$I_c = n\log_2 M \text{ (bits)} \qquad (3.5)$$

(Note: The bit is the smallest piece of information that can be stored on a computer and is a binary value of either 1 or 0. The byte is a unit used to measure the size of computer files, memory and storage capacity. One byte is made up from eight contiguous bits and stores the equivalent of one character. See Appendix A.)

As stochastic systems have only black and white levels, they have the same information capacity as a multilevel system with the minimum possible number of levels, that is, two. Using Eq: 3.1 and Eq: 3.5 it would seem possible to compare imagery between different systems, be they conventional photographs, or solid-state images (such as those made by a CCD imager comprising of $n$ MOS elements). And as this section of the book is intended to introduce and explain the complex nature of images (particularly digital systems) it is useful to see if information capacity correlates with perceived image quality.

For example, a 35 mm negative on Plus-X film might have something like $2 \times 10^5$ cells/cm$^2$, when calculated from a PSF at the 10% intensity level, which means a total of something like 1.7 million cells within the whole $24 \times 36$ mm format. And if we accept that Plus-X has three density levels ($10\sigma$), then the information capacity of this frame would be:

$$I_c = (1.7 \times 10^6) \log_2 3 = (1.7 \times 10^6)1.585 = 2.7 \text{ million bits}$$

But if we make $k$ equal to 4 rather than 10 standard deviations in Eq: 3.1, then our density levels are increased by a factor of 2.5 to yield $M = 7.5$, and the corresponding information capacity becomes 4.93 million bits.

By comparison, the Kodak DCS-420i digital camera (monochrome version) has $1524 \times 1012$ pixels framed in a chip of $14$ mm $\times 9$ mm, and 256 levels (although 12 bits are quoted, only the best 8 of these are employed). The information capacity of this system is given by:

$$I_c = 1\,542\,288 \times \log_2 256 = 1\,542\,288 \times 8 = 12\,338\,304 \text{ bits}$$

We can see that the digital camera is far superior in its information capacity! So much so, that the high data capture of these cameras can be a problem, and one that is usually solved by compressing the image to a much lower capacity before downloading it to a computer. But can we say that the image quality is better than that provided by Plus-X film? Perhaps as good (depending on enlargement) but, even when printed on a high-quality dye-sublimation printer and on the best glossy paper, the digital image will be hard pressed to better film—in terms of quality. However, this argument must also consider other factors, such as subject, lighting, presentation, etc. and, above all, the rapid improvements now being made to digital systems.

I think digital imagery is capable of reaching film quality— at a price! And when the capital outlay for high-quality digital cameras and supporting computer hardware becomes less, then the many advantages of digital systems will soon outpace those of traditional methods.

It is obvious that high values of $I_c$ are not enough on their own. From the above examples we can see that the Plus-X image will be improved as $M$ increases, but this cannot be extended without limit! Indeed, would the average observer really need 256 grey levels, or colours, in a photograph? Could he or she see more than, say, a 100, or appreciate more than 20 or 30? Would it not be better to adopt a stochastic system?

For monochromatic images stochastic systems work reasonably well:

> since at least two alternative states are required for the recording of information, maximum packing occurs when the cell is reduced to the size at which only two density levels are permitted by the granularity. Put in another way, maximum information packing on the photographic emulsion occurs for the case of binary (stochastic) recording. Brown, Hall and Kosar[11]

## Reciprocity between tone levels and resolution

In an experiment to determine the best compromise between regular/stochastic and regular/multilevel images, Metz et al.[8] illustrated a number of variants under each system. From their work they make it clear that 'information capacity and image quality are two very different quantities with no fundamental correlation between them.'

In their experiments they scanned a portrait photograph and reproduced facsimiles with varying amounts of $n$ and $M$. As might be expected, the quality of these reproductions improved with increasing the number of picture elements ($n$) and with increasing the number of grey levels ($M$). However, they found but limited reciprocity between values of $n$ and $M$. The best correlation (in terms of acceptable quality) was found to be between a stochastic image with $1408 \times 1216$ elements ($n$), and a multilevel image made up of $704 \times 608$ elements and 16 levels. As the reader can calculate from Eq: 3.5, both systems have equal capacity (1 712 128 bits) and although the stochastic image appeared rather 'grainy' it came close to the good-quality image provided by the 16 level system—even though the latter had less resolution.

## Regular/multilevel imagery

In Fig. 3.3 we have an interior photograph of a modern cathedral, and in Fig. 3.4, its scanned reproduction (Canon IX-4015). Held at some distance, or with the eyes screwed tightly enough to reduce edge definition of the pixels, the scanned image is almost passable with a resolution ($n$) of 64 pixels wide by 48 pixels high, and eight grey levels ($M$). From Eq: 3.5 the information capacity is 9216 bits. Obviously the scanned image has faults! Apart from its pixellated appearance the shadows are empty of detail and there is room for grey-tone improvement, but at a distance it will pass!

In Fig. 3.5(a) and (b), the same scanned image has been reproduced at one third the information capacity of Fig. 3.4, with noticeable effects. When viewed at sufficient distance to remove the obvious pixellation Fig. 3.5(b) approaches the quality of Fig. 3.4, but Fig. 3.5(a) is far too contrasty. The important feature of the two images in Fig. 3.5 is their reciprocity, for both have equal capacity at 3072 bits. In (a) the resolution is 37 pixels by 28 pixels with eight levels, giving $1024 \times 3 = 3072$ bits. Whereas in (b) we have a lower resolution of 32 pixels by 24 pixels with sixteen levels, giving $768 \times 4 = 3072$ bits.

The trade-off between resolution and grey levels is not a simple matter that can lead to global conclusions, particularly since other criteria are involved, such as viewing conditions, image contrast, 'graininess', pixellation, etc. But it remains obvious that given the largest possible number of $n$ and $M$ the image will always be at its best. As mentioned before, digital imaging systems involve a considerable amount of data

*Fig. 3.3* Photograph of an interior scene (a modern cathedral with daylight illumination).

*Fig. 3.4* Scanned image of Fig. 3.3 has a pixel resolution (*n*) 64 pixels wide × 48 pixels high, with eight grey levels (*M*). Information capacity $I_c$ = 9216 bits (binary digits).

storage and inevitably this puts a strain on tranmission systems and computer storage. In an attempt to determine the minimum practical number of data required to store and reproduce a recognisable image, I used a monochrome passport photograph of a college lecturer in an experiment to find the smallest value of $I_c$ that could be employed to reproduce a pixel picture with a 50% chance of the face being recognised among fifty of his students.

(a)

(b)

*Fig. 3.5* Images (a) and (b) have identical information capacity ($I_c = 3072$ bits). In (a) pixel resolution is 1024 pixels with eight grey levels, whereas in (b) resolution is only 768 pixels, but with twice the number of grey levels. Despite their reciprocity the images have a different appearance.

To begin with, the passport photograph was enlarged and the image analysed with a densitometer to divide the overall density range of the face into a number of nearly equal sub-ranges. Eventually, after a number of trials, four significant grey-tone levels were selected, and from four sheets of different grey paper a suitable pixel picture was mosaiced as shown in Fig. 3.6. With a crude resolution of only $15 \times 14$ pixels ($n = 210$) and four grey-tone levels, the information capacity came to 420 bits. Allowing each individual viewer an opportunity to observe the mosaic image at any given distance, it was found that 53% of the observers could recognise the face. A smaller sample was taken a year later with the stochastic version shown in Fig. 3.7, but on this occasion only 44% could recognise the subject.

These experiments were carried out many years ago and without the advantage of today's technology. It is now a simple matter to use a colour scanner, as shown in Fig. 3.8 (see colour section), where the original has been reproduced with $n = 374$ pixels and $M = 32$ colours, giving an information capacity of 1870 bits.

## 3.3 Spatial Resolution and Modulation Transfer Functions

It now seems common practice to discuss the resolution of digital imagery in terms of the sensor's packing density, that is, pixels per unit area or the number of pixels on the chip. This is certainly a useful form of discussing pixel resolution provided one can size the pixel-to-pixel distance. The Kodak M5 chip, as used in the DCS-420

*Fig. 3.6* Image of a face at minimum resolution ($15 \times 14 = 210$ pixels) and four grey levels provide an information capacity of 420 bits. Held at some distance with eyes screwed tightly the face becomes marginally recognisable.

*Fig. 3.7* A stochastic version of the face shown in Fig. 3.6.

camera, is a suitable example. This chip has an array of 1524 × 1012 pixels in an active area of 14 mm by 9.3 mm. between pixel centres. We can also state this as the sampling spatial frequency (ks).

$$k_s = 1000 / \Delta p \text{ (pixels/mm)} \tag{3.6}$$

where $\Delta p$ is the inter-pixel distance expressed in mm, and $k_s$ the sampling frequency.

## *Point spread function (PSF) and Airy discs*

The PSF shown in Fig. 3.1 illustrates the nature of an image point created on film, and in many ways is representative of most image points that are less than theoretically perfect. The PSF shown in Fig. 3.9 shows the symmetrical figure of an image point that can be found on the central axis of a good-quality lens—but it is not the theoretically perfect image point defined by what is known as the diffraction limited lens.

For a theoretically perfect image point, the PSF shown in Fig. 3.9 would be surrounded by an ever decreasing series of annular rings, known as an Airy disc (after the great astronomer of that name), and two such image points separated as shown in Fig. 3.10 would provide the limit for spatial resolution.

## *Rayleigh limited resolution*

The criteria for image resolution for a perfect (diffraction limited) lens is shown in Fig. 3.10, which shows that two Airy discs can be just resolved if the central maximum of one coincides with the first minimum of the other, the resulting dip in intensity between the two points being of the order of 18%.

The distance $r$ (the Rayleigh limit) is given in Eq: 1.12, but in practical terms can be approximated by:

$$r = \lambda N \tag{3.7}$$

where $\lambda$ is the wavelength of light employed, and $N$ is the relative aperture (*f* number) of the lens.

Although Eq: 3.7 suggests simplicity, we must remember that $\lambda$ represents a dominant wavelength out of a given bandwidth. For example, we might employ a filter

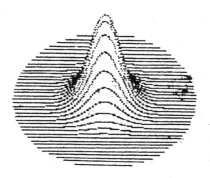

*Fig. 3.9* Point spread function (PSF) of a good image point.

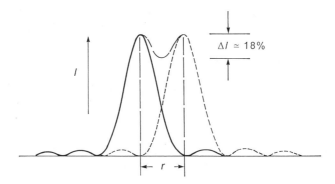

*Fig. 3.10* Image resolution (*r*) for a perfect (diffraction limited) lens. In practical terms $r = \lambda N$, where $N$ is the *f*/no of the lens.

which transmits between 480 and 540 nm, but its dominant wavelength could be 500 nm (0.5 mm). In this case, with a lens operating at *f*/4 ($N = 4$), the image resolution would be about 2 μm.

For the practical testing of spatial resolution it is usual to employ a simple square-wave type test target as shown in Fig. 3.11. The distance between the centre of one black line to the next being the same as *r* in Eq: 3.7.

The reciprocal relationship between resolving power (*r*) and image spatial frequency ($k_i$) is given by:

$$k_i = 1/r \text{ (line-pairs/mm)} \tag{3.8}$$

and if we combine the spatial frequencies of lens and sensor then, to a first approximation, we can put:

$$(1/k) = ((1/k_i)^2 + (1/k_s)^2)^{0.5} \text{ (line-pairs/mm)} \tag{3.9}$$

If we take a good-quality lens capable of providing an average resolution of, say 250 LP/mm, and if the sensor is Plus-X film with a known spatial resolution of 125 LP/mm then, from Eq: 3.9, we can calculate:

$$1/k = ((0.004)^2 + (0.008)^2)^{0.5} = \sqrt{((16 \times 10^{-6}) + (64 \times 10^{-6}))}$$
$$= \sqrt{(80 \times 10^{-6})} \approx 9 \times 10^{-3}$$

from which $k \approx 111$ LP/mm.

*Fig. 3.11* A square-wave test target. Black and white bars are of equal width.

Although Eq: 3.9 works reasonably well when the sensor is film there can be problems when the sensor is a regular array such as that found in CCD cameras.

## Nyquist sampling theorem

With sensors that have regular cell arrangements (such as CCD imagers—with spatial frequency $f_s$), unambiguous resolution of image detail with a spatial frequency $k_i$ > 0.5 $k_s$ is not possible since this would contravene the Nyquist sampling theorem.[12] The theorem states that the sampling of any signal that has a spatial frequency ($k_i$) close to the sampling frequency (or multiples thereof) gives rise to intensity modulations in the displayed image in the form of 'beats' between the two frequencies (i.e. $k_i \pm nk_s$), commonly called an 'alias' or 'moire' pattern. These are most noticeable about and above the Nyquist limit and arise because the intensity maxima and minima in the image do not always fully coincide with a sensor element. This is a fundamental limitation of all solid-state image sensors that have discrete sensor elements (such as CCDs) but as the spatial frequency of the sampling systems improves to higher values, so the problem becomes less important. The Nyquist limit is given by:

$$k_i \leq 0.5 \, k_s \qquad (3.10)$$

## Contrast and modulation

Contrast is simply the ratio of high intensity to low intensity, in either object or image. It can be expressed as:

$$C = L_h / L_l \qquad (3.11)$$

and can have any value. The contrast in the test target shown in Fig. 3.11 is very high, of the order of 100 : 1 or more.

Modulation, on the other hand, is a more useful parameter since it quantifies contrast with a scale that corresponds closely with that of visual perception. For example, there is little visual difference between a contrast of 100 : 1 and 1000 : 1, and this is shown by the small differences in modulation for these two contrasts. Modulation ($M$) is given by:

$$M = (I_{max} - I_{min}) / (I_{max} + I_{min}) < 1.0 \qquad (3.12)$$

For a contrast of 100 : 1, the corresponding modulation is 0.98, and for 1000 : 1 the modulation is 0.998, whereas for an average sunlit scene $M$ could be anything from 0.33 to 0.96.

## Analysis of a square-wave test target

Fig. 3.11 shows a simple square-wave target. But the image of such a target becomes less simple as we inspect its reproduction at higher frequencies (smaller scale). In Fig. 3.12, the upper diagram shows the ideal image of a square-wave target at spatial frequencies, 5, 10, 20 and 40 LP/mm. But the lower diagram illustrates the kind of reproduction we can expect!

It is obvious from Fig. 3.12 that whereas the lower frequencies only suffer degradation to the edges, the higher frequencies also suffer a loss of modulation.

## *Fourier analysis*

The square-wave form shown in Fig. 3.11 may be represented mathematically by a Fourier series composed of a fundamental sine wave (with the same spatial frequency $k$ as the square-wave target), plus a series of odd harmonics with spatial frequencies, $3k$, $5k$, $7k$, ..., $nk$. Indeed, a very close approximation to the square wave would result if the Fourier series were to be taken to enough terms. The square-wave function $f_x$ is given by:

$$f_x = 2(\sin x + \frac{1}{3}\sin 3x + \frac{1}{5}\sin 5x + \dots \frac{1}{n}\sin nx) \qquad (3.13)$$

In most types of photography (film), a microdensitometer trace across the image of a square-wave target seldom includes terms above the ninth harmonic, as shown in Fig. 3.13, where it may be seen that the sum of the first, third, fifth, seventh and ninth harmonics produces a rough approximation to the square wave (which has a mean height of $\pi/4$ of the first harmonic). Higher harmonics than the ninth are, generally speaking, removed by atmosphere, lens aberrations and the photographic emulsion until, at frequencies of about 5 LP/mm and higher, only the fundamental frequency is left in the signal.

Once the signal has been reduced to the fundamental frequency, we may consider square-wave targets to be effectively sinusoidal in character; and the only change left possible is for their images to be reduced in modulation, as shown by Fig. 3.12. If the original target could be made with a sinusoidal distribution of luminance, then the problem of harmonic stripping would not arise, and the difference between object modulation ($M_o$) and that of the image ($M_i$) would be the only variable involved. Although difficult to manufacture, sine-wave targets can be produced by photo-

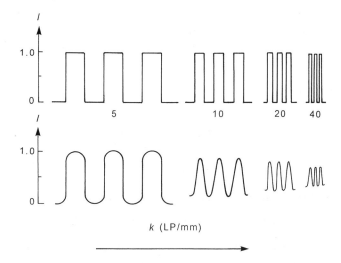

*Fig. 3.12* Top: an ideal square-wave target at spatial frequencies ($k$): 5, 10, 20 and 40 linepairs/mm. Bottom: their expected reproduction.

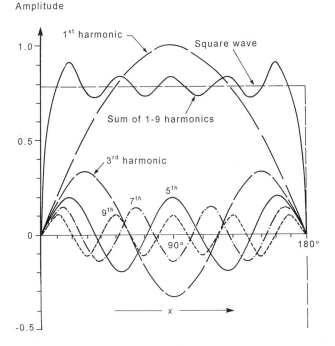

*Fig. 3.13* Fourier analysis of a square-wave target. The sum of odd harmonices (1 to 9) produces a rough approximation to the square wave at a mean height of $\pi/4$ of the first harmonic.

graphing a square-wave target with the aid of a cylindrical lens. An example is shown in Fig. 3.14 accompanied by its associated wave-form. Once again it is important to remember that the amplitude of light cannot be seen, and that intensity (which can) is proportional to the square of amplitude (Eq: 1.3). For a more comprehensive treatment of the Fourier approach to image formation the reader is recommended to read Saxby.[13]

## *Modulation transfer function (MTF)*

It is obvious from Fig. 3.12 that modulation in the object ($M_o$) suffers on transfer to the image ($M_i$), and for a given spatial frequency ($k$) the modulation transfer function (MTF) is given by the transfer factor $T_k$, where:

$$T_k = M_{i(k)}/M_{o(k)} \tag{3.14}$$

For a perfect (diffraction limited) lens the MTF is given by:

$$T_k = (2/\pi)(\pi/180)\cos^{-1}(k/k') - (k/k')(1 - (k/k')^2)^{0.5} \tag{3.15}$$

where $k$ is the spatial frequency for which $T_k$ has to be calculated, and $k'$ is the cut-off spatial frequency, given by $k' = 10^3/\lambda N$ ($\lambda$ in nm).

A family of diffraction limited MTF curves are plotted in Fig. 3.15 for a range of apertures (with $\lambda$ at 0.55 nm) along with the MTF for a Zeiss Pleogon air-camera lens.

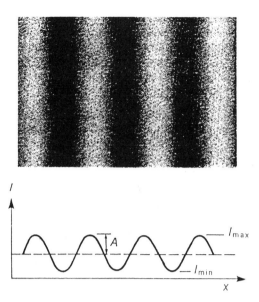

*Fig. 3.14* Sine-wave target.

A particular advantage of the MTF system is that it allows an entire system, that is, lens, sensor, atmosphere, image motion etc. to be cascaded (by algebraic multiplication of the individual values for each spatial frequency) to provide a total answer concerning the final image.[14]

## *CCD arrays: resolution and MTF*

Since we traditionally express optical resolution in terms of line-pairs/mm (Eq: 3.8) then we also need to equate the frequency of CCD pixels in much the same fashion (Eq: 3.6). A straightforward relationship would suggest that two pixels are equal to one line-pair, but in practice two pixels can often fail to resolve one black line and an adjacent white line (a line-pair). For this reason it has been suggested by Konecny, Schuhe and Wu[15] that a more reasonable solution is 2.8 pixels = one line-pair, and Makarovic and Tempfli[16] concluded (from MTF data) that 3.3 pixels would be needed to equal one line-pair. From these figures a compromise is recommended where:

3 pixels = one line-pair

Although the structural topography of CCD arrays will be discussed at length in Part Two, it can be said here that the active part of each CCD element (in which charges are located) is called the *channel* and this region is bounded by electrically inactive p-type *channel-stop* regions. The horizontal element spacing ($\Delta p$) is determined by the spacing of the charge transfer columns (as defined by the channel-stop regions) and the vertical pitch by the centre-to-centre spacing of the CCD elements. These limits provide the optical aperture of the elements ($w$), usually expressed in micrometres.

*Fig. 3.15* MTF curves for an ideal (diffraction limited) lens at three apertures, compared with the MTF of an actual air-camera lens.

If we employ a sinusoidal intensity target, such as that shown in Fig. 3.14, then the theoretical MTF of the sensor is given by:

$$MTF = \sin (\pi s(w /\Delta p))/(\pi s (w /\Delta p)) \qquad (3.16)$$

where $s$ is the 'normalised spatial frequency' ($s = k_i/k_s$).

In general there is little difference in the size of $w$ and the inter-element spacing $\Delta p$; consequently for all practical purposes we can put $w \approx \Delta p$ and the term ($w/\Delta p$) becomes unity.

A plot of MTF (Eq: 3.16) against the normalised spatial frequency ($s$) will approach 100% for relatively coarse image detail, that is, where $k_i < k_s$, and decreases as $k_i$ increases. At the Nyquist limit the MTF is reduced to 64%.

The MTF of a CCD image can also be degraded by inefficient charge transfer. It is a fundamental limitation of CCDs that, although charge is not lost, a small proportion of the charge signal is left behind at each transfer.[17] This residual charge adds to the next charge signal following through the array, which itself leaves a similar charge behind, and so on. As a consequence there is a loss of MTF which can be expressed as MTF′ and accounted for as:

$$MTF' = MTF \exp^{(-n\varepsilon(1-\cos(2\pi k_i/k_s)))} \qquad (3.17)$$

where:

$n$ is the number of transfers from point of charge generation to the output.

$\varepsilon$ is the fixed fraction of charge left behind at each transfer.

However, in modern buried channel CCDs (BCCD) the above effect is very small since $\varepsilon$ is only of the order of about $10^{-5}$.

# 4 Electrical Properties of Semiconductors

## 4.1 Electrical Conductors and Insulators

The resistance of conductors (as well as insulators and semiconductors) is partly determined by the number of electrons in the outermost energy level known as the *valence band* of the substance's constituent atoms (see Chapter 1). Under suitable conditions, such as the application of energy from an external source, electrons can be forced from the valence band into the even higher energy level of the conduction band. This transport of electrons is called an electric current.

In the case of a solid crystal the atomic nuclei are so close that the electrons of any given atom are influenced by those of its neighbours such that the energy levels (see Fig. 1.7) are broadened into bands of allowed values, grouped so closely together as to appear as a continuous band. Energy bands which electrons cannot occupy are called *forbidden bands.*

The maximum possible number of electrons in a valence band is eight, and an atom with eight valence electrons is normally an excellent insulator. This is because the valence band is filled, and may be considered to be in a state of equilibrium with a reluctance either to contribute or to receive an electron from the unfilled valence band of a neighbouring atom. All the inert gases (helium, neon, argon, krypton, xenon and radon) have eight valence electrons and are electrical insulators. But elements with six or seven valence electrons are also found to be good insulators, mainly because the gap between the valence and conduction bands is too great.

Atoms having only one, two, or three electrons in their valence band are usually very ready to accept electrons from, or contribute electrons to, neighbouring atoms and are therefore good electrical conductors. Metals like silver and copper have a single valence electron and make excellent conductors since they have a very small forbidden band—or none at all. When a battery is connected to a metal conductor some of the valence electrons gain a small amount of energy and move to the adjacent (unoccupied) higher energy level of the *conduction band* where they can move freely from atom to atom along the conductor. But with an insulator the valence electrons cannot gain sufficient energy from a battery to bridge the extremely wide gap to the conduction band. As a consequence there are no carriers available for conduction. Fig. 4.1(a) broadly illustrates these conditions for an insulator.

A basic electrical property of a material is its *resistivity* ($\rho$), which is a function of a material's *resistance* ($R$) given in ohms ($\Omega$), and the dimensions of that material.

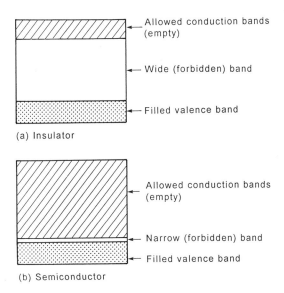

(a) Insulator

(b) Semiconductor

*Fig. 4.1* Typical energy bands for (a) an insulator, and (b) a semiconductor

From the well-known Ohms Law, which relates voltage ($V$) and current ($I$), we have:

$$R = V/I \quad \text{(Ohms)} \qquad (4.1)$$

We can then obtain $\rho$ from:

$$\rho = R\,(A/L) \quad (\Omega\,\text{cm}) \qquad (4.2)$$

where $A$ is the cross-sectional area in square centimetres, and $L$ is the length in centimetres.

Materials with values of $\rho < 10^{-2}\,\Omega$ cm are known as *conductors*; aluminium is an excellent conductor for example, and has a resistivity of $10^{-6}\,\Omega$ cm at room temperature. At the other end of the scale we have *insulators*, with values of $\rho > 10^5\,\Omega$ cm, Silicon dioxide, for example, has a resistivity of $10^{16}\,\Omega$ cm. In between these two types of material we have the *semiconductors*.

## 4.2 Semiconductors

Those elements with four electrons in the valence bands of their atoms, and compounds made up of one element with three valence electrons and another with five valence electrons, may be semiconductors.

Semiconductors are used to make solid-state electronic components, and some of these are light-sensitive devices that employ the *photoelectric effect*. One such photocell is the cadmium sulphide (CdS) photoresistor, which has a resistance that can vary from millions of ohms in total darkness to a few tens of ohms when illuminated. Another device is the metal oxide semiconductor (MOS) employed in CCDs.

Semiconductors have an energy band diagram similar to that of an insulator, but the gap between the valence and conduction bands is very narrow, as shown in Fig. 4.1(b). At absolute zero (zero degrees Kelvin) a pure semiconductor is an insulator, but at room temperature (about 20 °C, or 290 K) the mean thermal energy of an electron follows the expression:

$$E_t = 3kT/2 \qquad (4.3)$$

where:

$E_t$ is the mean energy of translation of a molecule,
$k$ is Boltzmann's constant, $1.38 \times 10^{-23}$ JK$^{-1}$ (joules per Kelvin),
$T$ is the absolute temperature of the molecule (in degrees Kelvin).

If we take a value for $T$ as 290 K, and since 1 eV = $1.6 \times 10^{-19}$ joules we can calculate the mean thermal energy of an electron at room temperature to be in the region of 0.04 eV. However, some of the valence electrons will have much more thermal energy than this, and can easily overcome the 0.75 eV forbidden energy gap of a germanium semiconductor, or the 1.1 eV forbidden gap of a silicon semiconductor.

Semiconductors are often 'doped' with controlled amounts of impurities so that the dopant lowers the resistance of the semiconductor to allow more current to flow through the device. If we introduce a pentavalent element (i.e. with five valence electrons), such as phosphorus, arsenic or antimony, into a pure silicon crystal (the host material, with four valence electrons) then each substitute atom has one more electron than necessary to make a covalent bond. These pentavalent atoms are called 'donors' since they donate an extra electron. And since they are not in a valence band, these excess electrons are free to carry a negative charge and leave behind a fixed positive charge (positive hole) in the substitute atoms. In this way the charge-neutrality condition is preserved. An absolutely perfect semiconductor is known as an *intrinsic* semiconductor where the concentration of electrons ($n$) and holes ($p$) are equal. Under these conditions an *intrinsic* semiconductor is not particularly useful, which is why dopants are employed.

Silicon doped with phosphorus is known as an *extrinsic* semiconductor of the negative type (n-type) because the concentration of free electrons is much larger than that of holes. If, on the other hand, a trivalent element such as boron, aluminium or gallium, is used as the substitutional impurity, a single electron is now missing from the bonding arrangement of elements, and a positive hole is produced with a fixed negative charge remaining in the impurity atom. Materials with an excess of holes are called p-type semiconductors. It is the movement of electron-hole pairs that carry the charge in solid-state junction devices.

The junction diode formed by an interface of p-type and n-type semiconductor materials is characterised by its ability to block the flow of electrons in one direction (reverse bias) while permitting electron flow in the opposite direction (forward bias). If electrons are directed into the p-type side of the diode they will not cross the interface of the pn junction, because the electrons already present in the n-type region repel them. But if electrons with sufficient energy are directed into the n-type side of the junction, they can easily cross over the junction to combine with the positive holes and create an electrical current.

It should be noted that all microelectronic devices make use of the pn junction in some form or other. While the operation of the diode described above is discussed in terms of electrons as carriers of electrical charge, it is also possible to consider the holes on the p-type side of the junction as being charge carriers, because holes continually migrate toward the pn junction to combine with arriving electrons.

The transistor is an important semiconductor component incorporating multiple pn junctions, and although there are numerous types of transistor they all allow a relatively large electric current flowing through the device to be controlled by a very small current or voltage at a third electrode, or gate.

## 4.3 Metal-oxide-semiconductor (MOS) Technology

Since the mid 1980s MOS technology has superseded the bipolar junction transistor both in sales and in applications, mainly through its simple structure and low fabrication costs. In this book it is important to discuss MOS structures since the MOS capacitor is basic to the charge coupled device (CCD), and although a silicon-silicon dioxide system is mentioned here, MOS technology is ever improving, and insulating materials other than pure $SiO_2$ are currently under consideration.[18]

### *MOS capacitor*

The basics of a MOS capacitor are shown in Fig. 4.2, where it can be seen that the structure comprises an aluminium gate (Al) over a dielectric material ($SiO_2$) deposited on a p-type silicon substrate. The band gap of the silicon dioxide insulator is 8 eV, and that of the p-type silicon semiconductor 1.1 eV.

As there is only a negligible voltage drop in the metal gate, the applied voltage $V_G$ is shared by the voltage across the oxide ($V_o$) and the *surface potential* ($\psi_s$), as:

$$V_G = V_o + \psi_s \qquad (4.4)$$

The surface potential is the voltage across the semiconductor, and by using the bulk Si as reference, $\psi_s$ can be considered as the potential at the Si–$SiO_2$ interface. For this reason it is known as the surface potential.

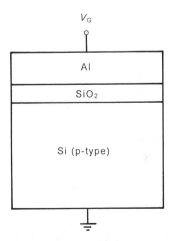

*Fig. 4.2* Basic MOS capacitor structure.

It should be noted that the SiO₂ layer is a good insulator and does not allow the conduction of current between the metal and semiconductor—even under bias, that is, as a dielectric the oxide will, under an applied electric field, cause a displacement of charge—but not a flow of charge.

Depending on the polarity and magnitude of the applied voltage, three different surface conditions are possible: (i) carrier accumulation, (ii) carrier inversion, and (iii) carrier depletion. Although all three conditions are important to the theory of the MOS capacitor,[19] it is the third condition that we shall consider here, since this allows us to explain the function of MOS elements in the CCD.

Fig. 4.3 shows a typical cross-section of a MOS capacitor. In this diagram the gate is shown as an aluminium type, but it could equally be a semi-transparent polycrystalline (polysilicon) gate as suited to a CCD imaging sensor. Other gate variants employed in CCD structures include polysilicon-aluminium, or two or three levels of polysilicon. Typically the SiO₂ layer will vary from a thin deposit of about 100 nm to a thick one in the region of 1 µm ($10^{-3}$ mm).

When a positive step voltage (up to about 10 volts) is applied to the gate of a MOS, the majority of carrier holes are repelled—resulting in a depletion region of negatively charged acceptor states under the gate, near to the surface of the silicon. In time, electron-hole pairs are generated in the depletion region, and electrons accumulate at the Si–SiO₂ interface to create an inversion layer, while the holes are driven to the substrate.

The surface potential ($\psi_s$) of a MOS capacitor, as a function of the applied voltage at the gate electrode ($V_G$), is given by:

$$\psi_s = V_G + Q_s/C_o \tag{4.5}$$

where:

$Q_s$ is the total charge per unit area in the semiconductor surface region (C/cm²),
$C_o$ is the SiO₂ capacitance (F/cm²).

The oxide capacitance ($C_o$) is given by:

$$C_o = K_o \, \varepsilon_o \, /x_o \tag{4.6}$$

*Fig. 4.3* Details of MOS capacitor with aluminium gate.

where:

   $K_o$ is the oxide dielectric constant (3.9 for silicon dioxide),
   $\varepsilon_o$ is the free space permittivity (F/m),
   $x_o$ is the oxide thickness.

Surface potential is also controlled by the substrate doping concentration, as well as the silicon oxide thickness.

## 4.4 Charge Coupled Devices (CCDs)

Essentially a charge coupled device is a silicon integrated circuit of the MOS type with a basic structure such as that shown in Fig. 4.4. A CCD comprises an oxide (SiO$_2$) covered silicon substrate upon which is formed an array of closely spaced electrodes. Signal information is carried in the form of an electric charge, usually electrons (although opposite polarity CCDs are also possible). The charge is localised under the electrodes with the highest applied potentials because the positive potential of an electrode ($V_G$) causes the underlying silicon to be in depletion (Fig. 4.3) and so assume a positive potential, which attracts the signal electrons. We can then say that the electrons are being stored in a 'potential well'. The active part of the CCD (where the charges are stored) is known as the channel, and this region is bounded by electrically inactive p-type 'channel stops' as shown in Fig. 4.4.

   The term 'charge coupling' refers to the method by which signal charges (which can be photoelectrons created from an image falling on the CCD array) can be trans-

*Fig. 4.4* Typical CCD structure.

ferred from under one electrode to the next. This is accomplished by taking the volt-age on the second electrode also to a high level, and reducing the voltage on the first electrode, as shown in Fig. 4.5. By sequentially pulsing electrode voltages between high and low levels, charge signals can be transported down an array of very many electrodes with hardly any loss and with very little noise. This CCD transport system is often compared to the action of a 'bucket brigade' used to convey buckets of water to fight a fire. This simile is made good by the fact that each 'bucket' is a potential well of electrons—carried along a 'shift register' to a final output.

## Three-phase CCDs

By connecting up three closely spaced MOS capacitors into storage elements, and applying a set of three-phase drive pulses $\phi_1$, $\phi_2$ and $\phi_3$ (typically from +5 to +15 volts), charge signals can be stored under every third electrode in each line of the array, as shown in Fig. 4.6. Under this system each storage element (or pixel if the input signal is optically generated) has every third electrode connected to the same clock voltage and consequently three separate clock generators are required, as shown in Fig. 4.6(a). If the positive voltage applied to $\phi_1$ is higher than that applied to $\phi_2$ and $\phi_3$, surface potential wells are formed under the $\phi_1$ electrodes, as explained for Fig. 4.5. Charge packets, introduced either optically or electrically, are accumulated in these depletion wells at $t = t_1$. These charge packets may be of different signal strengths. For example, those illustrated in Fig. 4.6(b) show the charge under gate 4 to be less than that under gate 1. It should be noted that the MOS capacitors must be close enough to allow their depletion layers to overlap; this is necessary so that the surface potential has a smooth transition at the boundaries of the neighbouring elec-trodes.

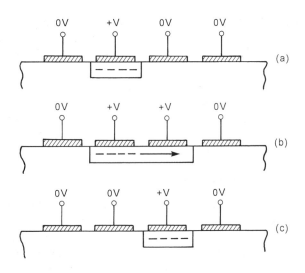

*Fig. 4.5* Signal transfer by charge coupling.

*Fig. 4.6* Three-phase CCD, showing storage elements (pixels) and drive pulses.

In order to move the charges to the right, a positive step voltage is applied to $\phi_2$ to ensure that the potential wells under the $\phi_1$ and $\phi_2$ electrodes are the same in depth. In this way the charge packets are allowed to spread out to the right, as seen at $t = t_2$, Fig. 4.6(c). Immediately after the pulse to $\phi_2$, the voltage at $\phi_1$ decays so that the potential wells under the $\phi_1$ electrodes slowly rise. The charge packets now spill over to the potential wells under gates 2 and 5 at $t = t_3$; see Fig. 4.6(d).

By repeating the same procedure the signals can then be moved from $\phi_2$ to $\phi_3$, and then from $\phi_3$ to $\phi_1$, and so on. At each full cycle of clock voltages the charge packets advance one storage element (pixel) to the right.

## Developments in CCD technology

It is perhaps appropriate at this stage to mention that the principle of the charge coupled device dates back to 1934[20] and since that time the CCD has developed from being a shift register memory store in computers to solid-state imaging systems. Bell Systems USA first announced the use of CCDs for a solid-state camera in 1972, and from there we had the well-known Sony Mavica in 1980. But it wasn't until the start of the 1990s that CCD technology had improved sufficiently to provide electronic imagery of good enough quality to interest people in its future as an alternative to film. Improvements are constantly being made of course, and it must be said that the technology mentioned in these pages can only provide a guide to the reader—in terms of future CCD developments. Indeed, some of the detail written here is likely to remain valid for only a few years at the current rate of technical progress! Nevertheless, it may be assumed that the basic theory will not alter too much, even as the fabrication of CCD imagers changes and improves at a steady pace.

Significant improvements already put into production include smaller storage elements, and a much higher pixel resolution of CCD imagers due to better fabrication techniques. There is also a continuous improvement in charge-transfer efficiencies and noise reduction through the use of *buried-channel CCDs*, and more advanced methods in clocking the electrodes using *two-phase* systems and *triple-polysilicon gates*.

Further improvements include semiconductor doping techniques, and the use of optical filters over storage elements to provide micro-colour pixels in the architecture of CCD imagers.

## Two-phase CCDs

Whereas in a three-phase CCD the potential wells are symmetrical, and charges can flow to either right or left, we have a much simplified system with two-phase clocking since the flow can only go in a single direction, as shown in Fig. 4.7.

To provide charge transfer with a two-phase shift register, potentials on adjacent electrodes are clocked between high and low levels (Fig. 4.7a) to direct charges to the right. A deep potential well (PW) which attracts electrons is formed under a 'high' electrode clock voltage and disappears under a 'low' voltage pulse. At $t = 0$ (Fig. 4.7b), $\phi_1$ voltage is high and the finite charge packet lies in the potential well under gate electrode 2 of storage element A. At a half-cycle time later (Fig. 4.7c), the potential well at gate 2 has collapsed due to $\phi_1$ going low, and the charge packet is now attracted to the new potential well under gate electrode 3, as $\phi_2$ goes high. At $t = 1$, the potential well under gate 3 has now collapsed with $\phi_2$ going low, and the electron packet moves to a new potential well under gate 4, which has gone high with $\phi_1$.

Usually we find that both two-phase and three-phase CCDs, employ optically transparent polysilicon-aluminium gates with an overlapping structure of the kind shown in Fig. 4.8.

## Buried channel CCDs

As we have seen from the previous diagrams, the CCDs described so far store and transfer their charges in potential wells situated at the silicon surface directly beneath the SiO$_2$ layer. For this reason they are known as *surface-channel CCDs* (SCCDs). But these surface states can adversely influence such things as transfer efficiency and noise levels—particularly if the signal strength is low.

A suitable arrangement for overcoming the worst of these problems is to fabricate what is known as a *buried-channel CCD* (BCCD). The buried channel is created by forming a diffused n-type layer on a p-type substrate, as shown in Fig. 4.8. If a large positive voltage is applied to the channel (via the input and output diodes) a depletion

*Fig. 4.7* Two-phase CCD. (a) Two-phase clock voltages. Stages of charge transfer are shown at (b), (c) and (d). PW - potential well.

layer is formed under the MOS capacitors. The potential well formed in the n-type buried channel will then store the signal electrons, which can then be transferred by the same clock pulses as used with SCCDs.

With BCCDs a transfer efficiency better than 99.99% can be achieved as well as higher clocking frequencies, up to 100 MHz.

## 4.5  Video Technology and the Digital Revolution

The term video was originally used in television to separate the picture from sound signals, but today it broadly refers to all systems that involve electronic imaging, including television, video cassette recorders (VCRs), camcorders and still video cameras. It is the last of these products that concerns us in this book, and although the

*Fig. 4.8* Three-phase buried channel CCD (BCCD).

term 'still video camera' is currently simplified to 'digital camera', we often find the former expression is still being used to differentiate digital cameras from camcorders.

As the technology moves forward, we find that many of the terms are either misunderstood or misplaced, and this is as much to do with a lack of standard terminology as it is careless advertising. Certainly we can class the digital camera to be part of video technology, but it has now grown out of its early origins, where a video (movie) camera was used to provide a 'still' image via an external device known as a *frame grabber*.

All video images are essentially in analogue form, that is to say, as electrical signals conveying luminance and colour with a continuously variable voltage. Up to the early 1970s television signals were almost all analogue. But as CCD and digital technology developed, much of the analogue video processing circuitry was replaced by high-speed sampling methods that convert continuously changing signal gradients into binary digits, each representing a discrete signal level.

The CCD camcorder was introduced in the latter part of the 1970s, and as a home-videotape camera it rapidly overtook the amateur cine camera, since it offered immediate access to the television screen. It also took on a professional role with outside television crews, electronic newsgathering, documentary filming and scientific recording. In the latter role there was a need for analysing certain frames and so the frame grabber was introduced to convert analogue signals into digital ones (A/D conversion), in order to grab a still picture (see Box 3).

**Box 3 Analogue-to-digital converter**

The analogue-to-digital converter converts analogue signals into a numerically equivalent form suitable for input to a digital computer. Analogue signals are of a continuously varying nature, but computers can only handle discrete bits of information. The A/D converter allows analogue data to be stored and handled by the computer with conversion rates as high as 1 GHz possible.

The required input voltages are the upper and lower reference voltages, the voltage to be measured and a clock pulse. The A/D converter comprises a series of binary voltage comparators supplied with the input signal and a reference voltage which is scaled between the low and high values. At each clock pulse the comparators are simultaneously read and a binary code is then generated, a process often referred to as *image quantisation*.

In short, an A/D converter is a register that can hold a digital value, an operational amplifier, and a series of binary voltage comparators. The register outputs are electrically summed to produce an electric current proportional to the digital value of the register. This current causes a proportional voltage gain at the amplifier output, and the amplified voltage is compared with the unknown input analogue signal. Provided there is a discernible difference, the voltage comparators allow the register value to change one step at a time until there is no difference. The register then holds the digital value equivalent to the analogue input.

A/D converters are common computer input/output devices used for control applications, and have resolutions that can vary from 8 to 14 bits. Frame grabbers usually have an A/D resolution of 8 to 12 bits (256 to 4096 grey levels). Conversely, computer produced control signals may require the complementary device, a digital-to-analogue (D/A) converter, for example for monitor display.

Usually a frame grabber is a printed circuit board fitted to a host computer, with its analogue entrance port matching the impedance of the incoming video signal which is then split into the synchronisation and analogue pre-processing modules. The A/D converter then translates the video signal into digital values by sampling the 0 to 0.7 V analogue voltage range and a digital image is constructed from each pixel, sampled at a rate based on the pixel clock and other synchronisation signals.

## 4.6 CCD Imagers

Often referred to as charge coupled imagers, digital cameras can take many forms, as we shall see in Chapter 5, but the main differences, apart from pixel specifications, centre on the type of sensor array employed.

So far we have concentrated on the basic mechanism of CCDs, but we must now look at the CCD imaging sensor in terms of its pixels (storage elements) which, as we have seen, can be formed by either two or three electrodes. Common to all CCD imaging sensors is the *photogate* (the optical window of the photosite) which is qualified by its *fill factor* or the percentage of the pixel that can be filled with light. These days manufacturers quote fill factors as high as 100% for some of their products.

At exposure to image light, each pixel will receive electrons in proportion to the incoming radiation and, as we have seen, each charge packet of electrons is then passed down the line of pixels by the process of charge coupling. Once a charge packet reaches the end of its line it is transferred to the output register and measured. It is important to remember that the signal received at the output register is in analogue form and remains so until put to the analogue-to-digital (A/D) converter. After A/D conversion each individual pixel receives a digital number (DN) according to its strength and corresponding to its sensor location within the array. (Note: The CCD's elements are only equivalent to pixels if the sampling rate at the A/D conversion is the same.) Naturally we can expect some of the charge to be lost at each potential well as the signal is passed down the line, but this is only a small amount with modern CCDs since they generally exhibit charge-transfer efficiencies as high as 99.99%, or one electron in $10^5$, a negligible amount when one considers that it takes over $10^5$ electrons to fill each potential well.[21]

The linear (one dimensional) array represents the simplest form of CCD imager and as such has been employed since the early 1970s in applications varying from space-bome military intelligence gathering to flat-bed scanners. A single line of CCD pixels are clocked-out into the parallel output register as shown in Fig. 4.9

However, in order to produce a two-dimensional image, a line array CCD imager has to be scanned, either by moving the array over the object, or vice versa. In aerospace imaging the former method is employed by a process known as *push-broom*, where the space vehicle or aircraft moves over the terrain and, akin to sweeping a floor with a broom, the linear array sweeps forward to scan the terrain in a regular pattern that is read out strip-by-strip via the output register into storage or direct transmission.

This technique has been instrumental in producing one of the earliest and most important forms of CCD digital imagery, not only for military reconnaissance but also for SPOT earth resources satellite cover, and airborne multispectral line-scan imagers such as the Canadian MEIS II SPOT for example employs linear arrays of 6000 ele-

*Fig. 4.9* A single-line CCD linear array.

ments in its panchromatic mode and 3000 in its multispectral mode (see Chapter 8) Similar methods are employed for flat-bed scanners, using either moving or static arrays.

## CCD area imaging arrays

Two-dimensional area imaging arrays come in two basic architectures today: (a) interline transfer, and (b) full-frame transfer. These array types continue to be manufactured and are subject to constant change and variation as the technology improves. The basic outlines considered here lack finite detail, but perhaps this is just as well, since there is little to be gained by detailing systems that are constantly in a state of change. Nevertheless, the two array types mentioned above are likely to remain as standard architectures for many years yet, with the full-frame transfer arrangement the most likely CCD architecture for current and future digital cameras.

### Interline transfer arrays

Interline transfer CCDs require twice as many pixels as a full-frame type, because columns of image sensors (pixels) are interspaced by columns of opaque transfer elements as shown in Fig. 4.10. Charge packets are accumulated in the sensor elements during image exposure, then shifted into the transfer columns and finally transferred, row by row, into the horizontal output (shift) register. The image is detected as two vertically interlaced modes and can be operated in either high resolution or standard television interlace mode. Interline transfer arrays are generally employed in the broadcast and home markets for video imaging systems, where they are favoured for their improved vertical resolution.

### Full-frame transfer arrays

The device must be considered as an array of horizontal pixels above a number of vertical charge transfer channels (or columns) defined by *channel stop* regions. At the

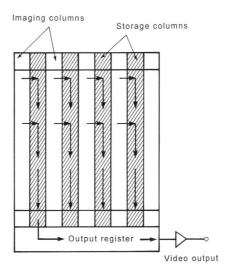

*Fig. 4.10* CCD interline transfer.

bottom is the 'line read-out' of the horizontal shift register, which transfers the charges in each pixel line to the video output amplifier. This amplifier is electrically shielded from the line read-out section by an output gate (OG) which is held at a (fixed DC) bias voltage ($V_{OG}$).

The clock pulses applied to *image,* and *shift register* sections are designated I$\phi$, and R$\phi$ respectively. Naturally the read-out sections are shielded from image illumination by opaque masking.

When the image section is illuminated, photons can pass through the semi-transparent polysilicon electrodes to generate electron-hole pairs within the silicon substrate. The electrons then diffuse to the nearest biased electrode where they are collected as a signal packet (Fig. 4.5) and the holes diffuse down to the substrate where they are effectively lost (Fig. 4.8). A single pixel is therefore an area bounded by the channel stops and the three (or two) electrodes centred on the biased electrode.

In the example shown in Fig. 4.11, there is a matrix of five pixels in each of eight rows, and the quantity of charge collected is proportional to the local radia-

*Fig. 4.11* CCD field-frame transfer array (after Hoare & Matthews, 1988). OG–output gate.

tion intensity and time allowed for collection, that is, the exposure time. At the end of the exposure time, the entire array of charges collected in the image array is transferred directly to the shift register. Normally the integrated charge detection amplifier is configured to provide a voltage output, where the output corresponding to each pixel ($V_p$) is proportional to the charge collected ($Q_p$). This can be achieved through a change of potential on the capacitance ($C$) of the charge detection node, that is,

$$V_p = Q_p/C \qquad (4.7)$$

It would seem that current developments favour a full-frame transfer array as the state-of-the-art architecture for modem digital cameras, the system is more efficient by improved clocking frequencies and the use of a mechanical shutter to prevent smear. Smear is a problem common to all types of frame-transfer systems and can be defined as the ratio between the change in image illuminance above or below a bright area covering 10% of the sensor extent in the column direction.[22] Smear is proportional to the ratio between illumination and transfer periods, typically in the region of 40:1. So, for a 10% extent on the sensor, the smear will be about 0.25% for a saturated image and would not be noticed normally. But if the image is over-saturated at any point, then the smear becomes apparent as 'image trails'.

All frame-transfer imagers can be illuminated either from the top through the senutransparent polysilicon gates, or through the back of the substrate providing it is suitably thin. Unfortunately thin wafer substrates are very fragile, as a consequence their use is generally reserved for CCD cameras that are attached to instruments such as astronomical telescopes and microscopes.

## CCD transfer efficiency

The fraction of charge transferred at each gate is called the *transfer efficiency* ($\varepsilon$). The fraction left behind, or loss-per-transfer, is designated with the symbol ($\alpha$). So the sum of these two components is given by:

$$\varepsilon + \alpha = 1.0 \qquad (4.8)$$

Since $\varepsilon$ determines how many transfers can be made before the signal output is seriously distorted and delayed, it is a highly important figure of merit for a CCD imager. If a single charge-pulse of amplitude $P_o$ is transferred down a CCD register with n transfers, the output will be:

$$P_n = P_o\, \varepsilon^n \approx P_o(1-n\alpha) \qquad (4.9)$$

When the product $n\alpha = 1.0$, then the original pulse is completely lost and distibuted among several trailing pulses.[23] Obviously $\alpha$ must be very small where a large number of transfers are required, as the following example makes clear.

If we consider a 1000 stage shift register and allow an overall loss >10%, then the product, $n\alpha \leq 10^{-4}$, and a transfer efficiency ($\varepsilon$) of 0.9999 is required.

For imaging applications the entire field of CCD stages are biased into deep depletion (Fig. 4.3), and then exposed to a focused image for a short period of time as the generation of carriers under a CCD gate is enhanced according to the image illuminance at that point. But there is a lower limit for the speed of operation of a CCD, where the signal has to be transferred into and out of a stage at a rate that is fast compared to the *dark current* generation rate at a depleted silicon surface. No stage in a CCD array can be held for a long time in conditions of deep depletion, and noise (such as that caused by dark current will be continuously added due to thermal generation. Most CCD signal charges usually range from about 10 to $10^7$ electrons. By comparison, a thermally generated dark current density of 1 nA cm$^{-2}$ corresponds to about 60 electrons per second under a 1 μm$^2$ gate.[24]

## *Dark current in CCDs*

Rather akin to the non-image light known as 'fog' in photographic films, *dark current* ($I_D$) arises from the thermal generation of electrons that accumulate in CCD elements and add to the photo-generated signals. A typical value is about 1% of the peak signal level ($I_p$). At 25°C, typical values are in the region:

$$I_P \approx 250 \text{ nA, and } I_D \approx 3 \text{ nA}$$

Ideally ID would be uniform—adding equally to the output of all pixels, but there will be some spatial variations due to inhomogenities in device manufacture, giving a 'pattern noise' that sets a minimum signal level below which imaging is not practical. It is also important to note that the dark signal and its non-uniformity are very temperature dependent and will generally follow the well known diode law:

$$I_D = Ae^{-V(bg)/(2 kT/q)} \tag{4.10}$$

where:

    $V_{(bg)}$ is the band gap for silicon ($\approx 1.1$ eV),
    $A$ is a constant,
    $k$ is the Baltzmann constant ($1.38054 \times 10^{-23}$ JK$^{-1}$),
    $T$ is the back-body operating temperature of the device (degrees Kelvin),
    $q$ is the charge of electron ($1.6021 \times 10^{-19}$ C) (Note: the coulomb = amp-second).

At normal room temperatures (20–25°C) we can expect values of $I_D$ to follow Eq: 4.10 quite well over the range –60 to 60° C. Using Eq: 4.10, with a known dark-current value of 3.5 nA for a device operating at 25 °C (298 K), the constant ($A$) is found to be 6.88, and when this value is inserted back into the equation values of dark current can be found for any other temperatures. Values of dark current relative to that found for 25 °C (3.5 nA) are shown plotted in Fig. 4.12, from which it can be seen that the *dark-current doubling-rate* parameter is a ± temperature shift of 9–10 °C.

Most of the current range of Kodak CCD image sensors have dark-current density values that are smaller than 10 pA/cm$^2$. But, as can be seen from Table 4.1, the *dark-current doubling rate* is now more sensitive at 5–6 °C, and for special applications, such as the long exposure periods required for astronomy or microscopy, special cooling down to –30 °C is required.

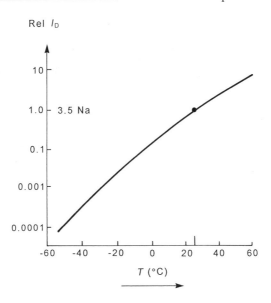

*Fig. 4.12* Typical example of CCD dark current (relative to that found for 25 °C, 3.5 nA) plotted against temperature.

*Table 4.1.* A sample of Kodak Full Frame CCD Imaging Sensors.

---

**Sensor: KAF - 1600 (Colour or Monochrome) 1.6 Million Pixels.**

Imager Size = 13.97 mm (H) × 9.29 mm (V).   Chip Size = 15.5 mm (H) × 10 mm (V).
Pixel Count = 1536 (H) × 1024 (V).   Pixel Size = 9 μm × 9 μm.
Optical Fill-Factor = 100% or 70% (colour).   Saturation Signal = 85,000 electrons or 40,000 (colour).
Output Sensitivity = 10 μV/electron.   Readout Noise (1 MHz) = 15 electrons RMS.
Dark Current <10 pA/cm$^2$.   Dark Current Doubling Rate = 5–6 °C.
Dynamic Range (Signal/Noise) = 72 dB.   Maximum Data Rate = 20 MHz.
Quantum Efficiency = 10% ($\lambda$ = 450 nm), 38% ($\lambda$ = 550 nm), 32% ($\lambda$ = 650 nm).

Applications: digital cameras, machine vision, astronomy and microscopy, aerial survey.

---

**Sensor: KAF - 6301 (Monochrome or Colour) 6.3 Million Pixels.**

Imager Size = 27.65 mm (H) × 18.48 mm (V). Chip Size = 29 mm (H) × 19.1 mm (V).
Pixel Count = 3088 (H) × 2056 (V).   Pixel Size = 9 μm × 9 μm.
Optical Fill-Factor = 100%.   Saturation Signal = 85,000 electrons.
Output Sensitivity = 10 μV / electron.   Readout Noise (10 MHz) = 15 electrons RMS.
Dark Current <10 pA/cm$^2$.   Dark Current Doubling Rate = 5–6 °C.
Dynamic Range (Signal/Noise) = 72 dB.   Maximum Data Rate = 10 MHz.
Quantum Efficiency = 10% ($\lambda$ = 450 nm), 30% ($\lambda$ = 550 nm), 40% ($\lambda$ = 650 nm).

Applications: digital cameras, inspection, film-scanning, astronomy, aerial survey.

---

*Table 4.1.* (continued)

**Sensor: KAF - 16801CE (Colour). 16 Million Pixels.**

| | |
|---|---|
| Imager Size = 36.7 mm(H) $\times$ 36.7 mm(V). | Chip size = 38.06 mm $\times$ 37.86 mm. |
| Pixel count = 4080 (H) $\times$ 4080 (V). | Pixel size = 9 $\mu$m $\times$ 9 $\mu$m. |
| Optical fill-factor = 70%. | Saturation signal = 650 mV. |
| Output sensitivity = 12 $\mu$V/electron. | Read-out noise 15 electrons RMS. |
| Dark current <10 pA/cm$^2$ @ 25 °C. | Dark current doubling rate = 5–7° C. |
| Dynamic range (signal/noise) = 71 dB. | Output Amplifier bandwidth = 80–120 MHz. |
| 2-Phase Register Clocking. | |

Quantum efficiency = 11% ($\lambda$ = 460 nm), 15% ($\lambda$ = 540 nm), 16% ($\lambda$ = 630 nm).

Applictions: digital cameras, studio, general, aerial survey, catalog, fashion.

(Kodak Product Specifications courtesy of Kodak Rochester USA.)

## *CCD noise*

There are three main sources of noise in CCD systems, and in their order of importance we can list them as: (i) photon shot noise ($N_s$); (ii) dark current noise ($N_s$) and (iii) circuit noise ($N_c$).

### *Photon shot noise*

Owing to the random arrival and absorption of photons, charge generation is a statistical process, and the *signal-to-noise ratio* (SNR) for the sensed image is at a maximum when the pixels are close to their full capacity (around $10^6$ electrons). Photon shot noise is given as the square root of the signal level (*S*), given in electrons:

$$N_s = \sqrt{S} \qquad (4.11)$$

### *Dark current noise*

As we have seen, dark current is produced continuously at a rate proportional to the absolute temperature (*K*) of the sensor material, and is generated at both exposure and read-out phases. Similarly, we find that if we measure the dark current ($I_D$) in electrons we have:

$$N_d = \sqrt{I_D} \qquad (4.12)$$

### *Circuit noise*

For a CCD sensor the largest source of circuit noise ($N_c$) is the on-chip amplifier, which is responsible for amplifying each individual pixel charge to a useful level. Subsequent to each pixel being p read-out, the amplifier must be reset to zero, and the uncertainty of the recovered zero level is known as *reset noise*. Reset noise *can* be kept low, but this depends on keeping the read-out speed very low. According to Janesick *et al.*[25] a specially constructed CCD imager (with 4096 $\times$ 4096 pixels) achieved sub-electron circuit noise levels, but requires 64 samples of each pixel and takes eleven minutes to read-out an entire image.

The sum of all the noise contributions is $N$, where.

$$N = (N_s + N_d + N_c) \qquad (4.13)$$

## Signal-to-noise ratio (SNR)

The signal-to-noise ratio for an imaging sensor is defined by the ratio between the signal and its noise, or $S/N$, where $N$ is the sum of the noise contributions listed above, i.e.:

$$\text{SNR} = S/N \qquad (4.14)$$

Usually expressed in decibels, Eq: 4.14 then becomes:

$$\text{SNR} = 10 \log(S/N) \text{ decibels} \qquad (4.15)$$

Obviously noise becomes a problem mainly at low image–intensity levels, where the signal ($S$) is close to the overall noise level (*noise floor*). But as the charge capacity of the pixels increases so does the SNR and the dynamic range of the image.

All CCD image sensors have a maximum output signal (or saturation level) and a root mean square noise threshold, with voltage: $V_{sat}$ and $V_{N(rms)}$ respectively. The characteristic linear response region of the imager lies between these two levels, and when CCD analogue signals are quantised into a binary scale, the dynamic range of the image is typically defined as the ratio between the two levels. Expressed in decibels the dynamic range (DR) is given as:

$$\text{DR} = 20 \log (V_{sat} / V_{N(rms)}) \text{ decibels} \qquad (4.16)$$

Note: Most modern CCD imagers incorporate a lateral overflow drain to prevent *blooming,* a common problem where excess charge is drained off from bright pixels that are over illuminated. Blooming is the major cause of poor highlight resolution.

## CCD Linearity

As can be seen from Fig. 2.9, the CCD sensor is capable of generating electronic charges in direct proportion to the incident illumination. This is an ideal imaging system, unmatched by any conventional photographic process, and providing the CCD signal does not suffer from non-linear features in the amplifier circuit, the output signal ($S$) from a pixel can be given by:

$$S = kq^{\gamma} + I_D \qquad (4.17)$$

where:

$k$ is a constant of proportionality,
$q$ is the generated charge,
$I_D$ is the dark current signal.
The sensor output is linear when $\gamma$ is equal to unity.

# 4.7 Complementary Metal Oxide Semiconductors (CMOS)

Both CCD and CMOS are built from silicon, and have similar sensitivities over the visible and near-infrared spectrum. Both technologies convert incident photons into electronic charge (electrons) by the same photoconversion process, but there the similarity ends. CMOS technology is far more economic in production and requires only one chip (the CCD requires at least three) virtually all of the electronic camera functions can be integrated on the same chip giving rise to the expression '*camera on a chip*'. The CMOS requires only a third of the power (e.g. 3.3 V) of equivalent CCD imagers, and is far cheaper to produce, while making a more compact camera it was thought that it provided an ideal product for the *low end* of the market. But recent developments and commercial interests have shown that CMOS is rapidly becoming a threat to CCD dominance in the *mid* to *high end* of the popular market.

In the past the main drawback of CMOS has been the question of resolution, and noise, although it seems to have overcome the main objections of these, and now it would appear they are no longer valid. Shipments of CMOS by the year 2005 are expected to exceed those of CCDs

The CMOS imagers sense light in the same way as CCD, but from here on everything is different. The charge packets are not transferred, as with the CCD, but are detected immediately by charge sensing amplifiers which are made by CMOS transistors as shown in Fig. 4.13. Some CMOS sensors have an amplifier in every pixel as in Fig. 4.14, these are called *active pixel sensors* (APS), usually APS contain at least three transistors per pixel. In general, each photosite contains a photodiode converting light to electrons, a charge-to-voltage conversion section, a reset and select transistor and an ampifier section. Overlaying the entire CMOS sensor is grid of metal connections to apply timing and read-out signals, and an array of column output signal connections. The column lines connect to a set of decode and read-out electronics that are found by each column outside of the pixel array. Because the pixels in CMOS imaging arrays are 'read out' in parallel, row by row, they are much faster than CCD arrays that read out pixels sequentially, and because CMOS draws much less power than CCDs it allows the camera to run longer on batteries, a very significant advantage.

There are an increasing number of high end digital cameras which use CMOS technology, such as the Canon EOS D30 (2001) 3.1 MPx (2160 × 1440 pixels) which is priced at £2000. With a rather slow speed rating of 100 ISO, it can be uprated to 200 without any real difference, until 400 ISO when noise becomes quite noticeable. Then in 2002, we have the Canon EOS D60 model at the same price using the less expensive CMOS but with 6.3 MPx output! The pixel count is 3072 × 2048 pixels, and the results are considered superb. Then we have the Kodak DCS Pro 14n which is due on the market December 2002. All three are SLR cameras, with all the sophistication that is expected of such, built from Nikon parts the Kodak DCS Pro 14n will sell for about £3200 and is fully compatible with the entire range of Nikkor lenses. Using a CMOS chip the DCS Pro 14n can rival CCD imagers, and CMOS was chosen to keep costs down, due to the economy of scale of CMOS manufacturing plants.

## 4.8  Foveon X3 CMOS Image Sensor

If the concept of increasing CMOS technology is something of a break-through in image technology, then Foveon's colour recording system is truly dramatic. The Foveon X3 CMOS has three photosites arranged vertically in each pixel to capture the red, green and blue wavelengths at every point instead of separately using filters. Rather than using a Bayer filter method for isolating each colour, the X3 solution

(a)

(b)

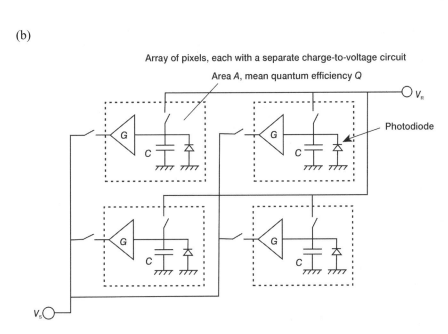

*Fig. 4.13* A CMOS sensor with an amplifier on every pixel.

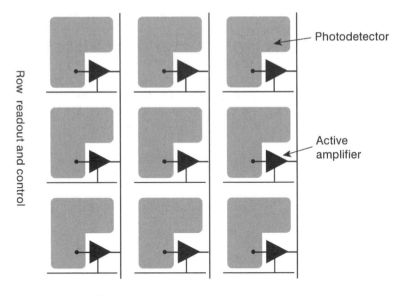

Row readout and control

Photodetector

Active amplifier

Column readout and control

*Fig. 4.14* The principle of the Foveon X3 CMOS image sensor with vertical RGB recording.

relies on the different wavelengths penetrating to different depths in silicon, where they can be detected individually. The principle of vertical photosites relies on the fact that silicon absorbs RGB at different depths: the short blue waves barely penetrate to about 20 nm, the longer green waves to about 200 nm and the red wavelengths to about 500 nm, as per Fig. 4.15. The three charges are then sent sequentially to sep-

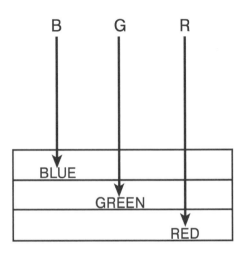

B  G  R

BLUE

GREEN

RED

*Fig. 4.15* The Foveon ×3. A CMOS image sensor with vertical RGB recording. The silicon absorbs RGB at different depths.

arate colour integration circuits in each pixel, and held there until read-out, when the colour voltages are applied to the output column.

The Sigma SD 9 is the first camera to use the X3 CMOS sensor, with 3.5 MPx (2268 × 1512 pixels) each pixel has three photosensors to record each of the RGB colours, the output should therefore have as much data as a 10 MPx normal sensor. In addition, the X3 is collecting information from a smaller area resulting in the sensor having greater resolution. The Sigma SD 9 is a conventional SLR with a shutter speed varying from 30 seconds to 1/6000, it is priced around £2000.

# 5  Digital Cameras

## 5.1  Introduction

Although a number of CCD imagers had been produced as a variety of research tools by the late 1970s, the general public only became aware of the electronic camera when the Sony Mavica camera was exhibited at Photokina (Köln, Germany) in the latter part of 1980. It had a phenomenal impact on those who, like me, saw the Mavica demonstrated—but, despite the many claims made for this camera, neither the market, the media nor the public were ready for such an innovation. There were notable exceptions of course, particularly from Geoffrey Crawley, the far-seeing editor of the *British Journal of Photography*, who had been warning the photographic profession of the CCD future for a number of years and who, in 1972,[26] published a first class account of how a CCD imager worked. This article was republished in 1981 with a review of the Mavica[27] and was immediately followed with a further view on the future of solid state imagery a few weeks later.[28]

But although there was some enthusiasm for CCD imagers it was all too premature! Even if the Mavica had gained the necessary financial support, the market was reluctant to press photographers into purchasing an expensive camera that was really no more than a 'freeze-frame video' system with the limited image quality of 570 (horizontal) × 490 (vertical) pixels. As Crawley rightly pointed out in 1981:

> *'That announcement of a prototype solid-state imaging camera by Sony should cause nervousness and apprehension is very difficult to understand, especially when one considers that electronic imagery will only broaden the whole scope of photography and its associated industry and trade.'*

One can understand the reluctance of both professional and amateur photographers to take on board an unproven system that offered much less than their conventional cameras. But as Crawley put it in 1981:

> *'The Sony Mavica and its like have nothing to offer the professional except early notice that over the next decade new methods and techniques must be learned—the Journal has been warning about this for years, so it should not come as a surprise.'*

How right he was! At that time, I was teaching CCD imagery to students studying for a degree in Photographic Sciences—but again, it was too early, and without the practical support of an available CCD camera there was little or no interest from either colleagues or professionals.

The Mavica looked like an ordinary 35 mm camera, but loaded a flat 50 mm diameter floppy disk instead of film. According to announcements some fifty colour images could be stored on the magnetic disk, which could then be downloaded into a Mavica viewer or television set. It must be remembered that the Mavica was not a digital camera: the images were strictly analogue! And for all its promise it was never marketed—not too surprising in hindsight, since the personal computer (PC) and essential peripherals were only in their infancy at this time. In the meantime, while the major photographic manufacturers started to research and develop digital cameras in earnest, few people thought there would be any major developments for at least a decade—a prediction that was mainly true!

## 5.2 Basic Types of Digital Camera

There are several types of 'digital' camera, and all of them are still in production since they offer various advantages according to application and cost. One can also predict that there will be many further types as technology improves, but it is likely these will only be variations of those designs with popular and economic appeal.

The list of digital camera designs given in Table 5.1 is not exhaustive, but simply shows the various methods of achieving a digital image with a camera designed for a particular role. Image quality, in terms of spatial resolution, colour fidelity and dynamic range, always have to be balanced against cost, operating facilities (such as range of available lenses, shutter-speeds, apertures, number of images, frame recycle time, etc.) and compatibility with computer hardware and software.

In Table 5.1 it must be noted that the name used to describe a given type of imager may well be different from that used by a manufacturer; nevertheless it is hoped that the description of the type's technology will suffice to avoid any confusion.

Although some of the types listed in Table 5.1 are rather specialised and often highly expensive, the range of instrumentation is rich enough to support numerous innovations for the future. Already there have been about 3000 different cameras manufactured and marketed, not including the special types made for scientific and industrial work. Indeed, the growth of this young industry is so rapid that it is almost impossible to keep up with the changes now being made.

It is obvious that the high price of a reasonable quality digital camera must fall significantly before it can compete with its film counterpart. This is sure to happen within the space of a few years of course; meanwhile the market is being flooded with what are known as *low end* cameras in the £50 to £300 range in order to stimulate interest among those who appreciate their potential. The keen amateur photographer has long been able to satisfy his/her hobby from a need to provide photographic records at the workplace. Professionals in every walk of life (scientists, medics, engineers, teachers, surveyors, estate agents, police officers, technical authors, …) have all been used to providing their own photography for many years—thanks to conventional SLR camera technology and a high-street chain of colour processing outlets. But these same users are also among some 70% of UK households who either own or

Table 5.1 Basic types of digital camera design

| | Design type | Description | Major application |
|---|---|---|---|
| 1 | Single exposure single area-array | Spatial multiplex system. Low-to-high definition (monochrome & colour) | Hand-held general and scientific work. CCD & CMOS. (e.g, *DCS-760*) |
| 2 | Single exposure single area-array, vertical colour photo-sites | RGB wavelength absorption at different depths in each pixel. No interpolation of colour necessary | Hand held general and scientific work. CMOS Foveon *X3* |
| 3 | Single exposure three area-array chips | Parallel acquisition via three RGB filters, beam-splitter. (monochrome & colour) | Studio high quality, fashion advertising, etc. (e.g, Minolta *RD-165*) |
| 4 | Three exposures single area-array | Temporal multiplex system via spinning three-filter disk (monochrome & colour) | Studio high quality, fashion advertising, etc. (e.g, Leaf *Volare*) |
| 5 | Scanning linear-array, push broom or static array | Scanned CCD (1 or 3 CCD linear-arrays). Monochrome or colour | Studio CCD cameras, aerospace systems, flat-bed scanners. (e.g, Agfa *StudioCam*). |
| 6 | Scanning CCD-back for studio cameras | Scanned linear-array, 'slip-in' type camera back. 70 mm or 5" × 4" monochrome & colour | Studio high quality digital option. (e.g, Leica *S1*) |
| 7 | Single exposure single area-array camera-back | Single exposure 'slip-in' type camera back 70 mm or 5" x 4" monochrome & colour | Studio or general work for medium format cameras (e.g, Kodak *DCS 465.* 6MPx) |

have access to computers (of which only 10% are Macintosh, the majority being IBM compatible PCs), and their ability to use these computers and their peripherals also gives them an opportunity to engage with digital imagery—without the need for dark-rooms, chemicals and other inconveniences.

The so-called low end cameras (among those listed as Type 1 in Table 5.1) satisfy numerous requirements, where quality need not be as good as that provided by conventional means. They can provide images of a suitable resolution for purposes such as industrial and commercial reports, technical notes, house agent leaflets of property sales, police records and direct communications via fax or Internet. They are not of sufficient quality to satisfy most commercial or advertising requirements, and are not usually suitable for top-quality brochures and journals, but these needs are taken care of by the *high end* digital cameras costing anything from about £5000 to £25 000. As may be expected, these high end cameras are relatively few because of their high cost, and the fact that their exposures are usually counted in minutes rather than fractions of a second. The important system configurations listed as Types 1, 3 and 4 (Table 5.1) are shown in Fig. 5.1.

All this leads us to the more interesting *middle range* of professional digital cameras (to be found in the *spatial multiplex* systems under Type 1 of Table 5.1) currently priced between £1000 and £13 000. These must surely represent the primary concern of both manufacturers and users alike. The prime market rests with these middle range types, where one-shot, colour imagery of photographic quality can be attained with SLR type cameras. Such cameras already exist—and the price is quite reasonable, such as £969 for the Nikon 5700, or £2000 for the Canon (CMOS) EOS D60, or £4400 for the Canon EOS 1D, up to the £13 000 for the Kodak Pro Back fitted to the 555ELD Hasselblad.

(a) Spatial multiplex system     (R = red, G = green, B = blue)

(b) Parallel acquisition system

(c) Temporal multiplex system

Single CCD sensor

*Fig. 5.1* Three types of CCD imaging systems.

# 5.3 Single Exposure, Single Area-array (Spatial Multiplex) Cameras (Type 1)

These cameras are the most well-known and popular type of digital imager today, mainly because they operate in much the same fashion as conventional cameras, except that a two-dimensional area-array CCD imager replaces the film.

This type of camera supports much of the full-frame area-array technology mentioned in Chapter 4 and provides a sound basis for future developments. Indeed, hardly a month passes without a new model coming on the market, many of these being modified conventional 35 mm cameras such as the SLRs manufactured by Nikon, Fuji and Canon, with the CCD or CMOS chip and imaging algorithms provided by another company, such as Kodak. As we have seen in Chapter 4, monochrome area-array imagers have a spatial resolution accorded by the $x$, $y$ pixel density. In general pixels are square shaped with sides of 9 μm.

Eastman Kodak are a major provider of CCD imaging chips, such as the KAF-6301 full-frame CCD (usually referred to as the M-6 chip) incorporated in the DCS-560, DCS-660 and DCS-760 models costing around £14 000 for the first two and half that price for the DCS-760. Full details of these chips can be found in Table 4.1.

Although there are numerous variations with each type of digital camera, many currently follow an almost basic pattern for image capture. Typical of Type 1 cameras is the Kodak DCS-760, which is priced at £6900. In this respect it represents the professional range of Type 1 digital cameras very well.

Although practical specifications of digital cameras are published, full technical data, such as that freely available for conventional cameras, is almost impossible to find. There are good reasons for this of course. Whereas conventional cameras have little to offer that is radically new, every fresh digital camera usually incorporates something unique by way of innovation or advanced technology. As a consequence all manufacturers are reluctant to disclose their secrets—even if in reality they are not secret at all! Naturally much more will be revealed—but slowly—during the years ahead. At this time, however, what *is* known (or thought to be known) about a given digital camera is usually a mixture of truth, conjecture and advertising.

## *A typical area-array digital camera system*

We have seen (Fig. 4.11) how the CCD area-array image is captured, and have discussed how analogue image information is sent to an A/D converter via the output register on the CCD chip. From this point onward the rest of the story takes place inside the camera, within the computer and in the software.

As mentioned, each digital camera has its own system, and although many follow a typical structure and circuitry, the necessary mathematical algorithms that control such things as image compression and colour interpolation are usually unique to a specific camera and associated software.

If we define the archetypical digital camera as one which employs a high-quality SLR camera with an area-array CCD sensor that can provide near photographic quality (in colour), to a diverse population of professional users, then the Kodak DCS-200 camera should take the honours as being the first major success in its field. Although not the first digital camera to be formed from a well-known SLR, it was at least a 'stand alone' system and in this respect a great advance on its (1991) predecessor, the DCS-100. The Kodak DCS-100 was based on the Nikon F3 body and was suitably compact—but in use the camera had to be interfaced with a large external digital storage unit (DSU) carried as a shoulder pack. The DSU also incorporated an inch monitor to display each of the 156 uncompressed images. The camera was designed for photo-journalists, and could be supplied with built-in image compression (400 to 600 images with JPEG compatible compression) to allow news pictures to be sent down telephone lines to the news desk. (JPEG is a standard compression and stands for Joint Photographic Experts Group). Such additional (and relatively heavy) burdens as the DSU do not generally endear themselves to itinerant photographers however, and so it was not surprising to see the self-contained DCS-200 camera introduced in 1992.

## *History of the Kodak DCS-200 digital camera*

The Kodak Digital Science Camera 200, complete with the M-5 chip housed within a Nikon 801s (N8008s USA) camera body, was an immediate success. With a 1.5 million pixel resolution, an exposure recycle time of three seconds, and a capacity of 50 compressed images stored in an 80 Mb hard disk, the DCS-200 was a leader in its field. As such, although replaced by the more advanced DCS-420, and the 6 MPx DCS-460, the DCS-200 serves as an excellent example for further discussion of its type.

Although larger and heavier than its host camera, the DCS-200 is still a very compact unit, as may be seen from Fig. 5.2a. For any necessary servicing the digital back can be removed to reveal the CCD sensor, as shown in Fig. 5.2b. The front view of the digital back can be seen in greater detail in Fig. 5.3a, and its rear view (Fig. 5.3b) shows the various controls and a SCSI (an acronym, pronounced *scuzzy*, which stands for 'small computer system interface') port for connection to Macintosh or PC.

The DCS-200 was manufactured in a number of versions. The basic model 200 was monochromatic and came without an internal hard disk. Then there was the DCS-200c, the colour version; and the most expensive version (at £8500): the DCS-200ci with colour and hard disk. All models have the same chip, but the colour version has mosaiced RGB colour filters overlaying the pixels. The M-5 chip with dimensions 14 mm × 9.3 mm contains a matrix of 1524 × 1012 pixels in a full-frame area-array imager. Each of the 1 542 288 pixels are 9.2 µm square and have a spectral response that extends usefully into the near infrared, as shown in Fig. 5.4.

Apart from the four usual batteries that power the Nikon 801s camera, the digital back operates from six AA type rechargeable NiCd batteries. When the camera is awake, the *battery indicator* (shown by the liquid crystal display (LCD) Fig. 5.3b) displays the current battery life, with the bottom indicator blinking to warn when battery life is exhausted. The same LCD provides a *frame counter, disk indicator* (to inform how much hard disk space is left), *frame-delete indicator, SCSI connection indicator* and an *ISO warning indicator*. The ISO warning indicator refers to the four prescribed ISO settings on the camera back, and since the DCS-200 can provide images at only one of the prescribed ISO values, the LCD will display 'ISO' if the camera has not been set either to: ISO 50, 100, 200 or 400 for colour work, or to ISO 100, 200, 400, or 800 for black and white photography.

Kodak DCS-200 Digital Camera.    Kodak Digital Back.

Nikon N801s Camera
(with film-back removed)

(a)                    (b)

*Fig. 5.2* The Kodak DCS-200, incorporated with the Nikon N801s host-camera: the first of a highly successful series using the M-5 sensor. (From the Kodak DCS-200 manual.)

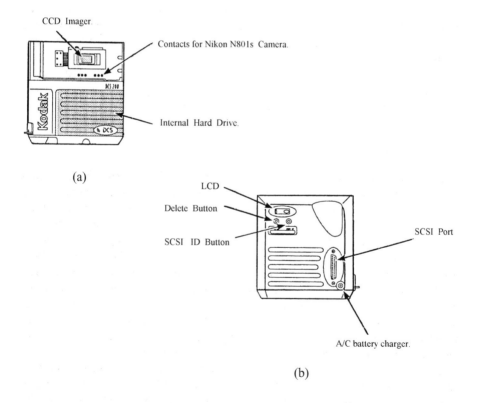

CCD Imager.

Contacts for Nikon N801s Camera.

Internal Hard Drive.

(a)

LCD

Delete Button

SCSI ID Button

SCSI Port

A/C battery charger.

(b)

*Fig. 5.3* The DCS-200 digital camera back. The M-5 CCD sensor has a matrix of 1524 × 1012 pixels, each 9.2 mm square, within a 14 mm × 9.3 mm format. (From the Kodak DCS-200 manual.)

*Fig. 5.4* Spectral response curve for the M-5 CCD sensor.

The digital back also incorporates two control buttons: *Delete* and *SCSI ID* (Fig. 5.3b). The Delete button allows the operator to delete the last image on the hard disk, and the SCSI ID button is used to select the correct ID value on the camera as used by the PC.

The following descriptions (based on the DCS-200, with uncompressed images) provide a notional explanation of the image route taken by both monochrome and colour CCD imagers and will it is hoped give the reader a reasonable grasp of the digital image route from camera to screen.

### *Monochrome image route*

Once a picture has been taken with a monochrome CCD imager, each image point is then clocked-out, pixel-by-pixel, along the *shift register* to the *output amplifier*, and then to an 8 bit A/D converter where each pixel-charge value (along with its $x$, $y$ location) is registered in the form of a binary code. From here the image data are temporarily stored in an 8 bit *buffer memory* before being sent to a programmable *digital signal processor* (DSP) where the image is stored with other data in the 2 Mb of *dynamic random access memory* (DRAM). Once the data are in the single-frame DRAM, the camera's hard disk is started and image data transferred to it. Hardware in the camera's digital back generates a *thumbnail*, which is a subsample of image data, with data sampled from every eighth pixel. The thumbnail is subsequently stored with the full image on the hard disk. This process takes just over three seconds on the DCS-200 before the camera is ready to expose another picture.

After the image data (up to a maximum of 80 Mb) have been stored on the camera's hard disk, the digital data can then be downloaded to the computer (via the SCSI) where they are received by the manufacturer's image acquisition software. From this stage in the image route the picture may then be saved into any file format supported by the TWAIN (Toolkit Without An Interesting Name—believe it!) compatible host software, such as the highly popular Adobe® Photoshop® variants now at large.

Finally, the image-processed data are then sent to the computer monitor's DAC (digital-to-analogue converter) which does the reverse job of the digital camera's ADC (analogue-to-digital converter). This conversion is necessary since the monitor only accepts analogue signals (as a stream of rapidly varying voltages) that need to be continuously refreshed at the VESA (Video Electronics Standards Association) rates of 72 Hz. Alternatively, the image can be sent to a printer to provide a hard copy.

## Colour image route

For colour work the CCD imager must be modified if it is to be of the type shown in Fig. 5.1a, that is, of the *spatial multiplex* type. This is a popular system as it allows for single exposures and virtually makes the camera little different from convention-al film types. The technique is to provide an individual red, green or blue filter over each pixel, in much the same way as the additive colour process used by Agfa in the 1930s. The mosaic chip pattern shown in Fig. 5.5 (see colour section) is only one of many CFAs (colour filter arrays) now in current manufacture, and illustrates the typ-ical repeating $2 \times 2$ matrix that uses two green cells for every single red and blue cell. Although this arrangement is now common for many imagers (known as the Bayer filter array, after the Kodak scientist of that name), there are other configurations that employ quite different matrixes. The reason for the two-to-one ratio of green cells is to provide for improved green sensitivity so that the image will parallel the response of the human eye, as shown by Fig. 2.1.

Known as the *adjacent pixel colour interpolation technique,* area-array systems ensure that each pixel filter is always adjacent to the other two. Because each pixel has to be able to record all three RGB colours, camera software looks at the strength of the missing colours recorded by adjacent pixels, and makes a qualified evaluation of the two missing colours on a pixel-by-pixel basis. If, for example, the camera was to record a uniform red object, it would not be just the red-filtered pixels that created a charge signal, but *all* of the pixels red, green and blue! Were this not so there would be open gaps in the resolution.

All of the pixel filters are broad-band types, allowing certain amounts of other colours through, that is, red-green and blue-green; consequently the software algo-rithm has some signal information on each pixel regardless of the image colour at that point. In the example of the uniform red image, the interpolation algorithm finds lit-tle response in the green, and even less in the blue-filtered pixels, and since the entire matrix in the immediate area has the same response the algorithm calculates a totally red image at this point.

The method of colour interpolation degrades spatial resolution by a factor of $\sqrt{3}$ and, as outlined in Chapter 3, if three pixels are equal to one line-pair, we can put the spatial resolution of a monochrome CCD imager as:

$$r_{mono} = 3 \text{ px} \quad (\mu m) \tag{5.1}$$

and

$$R_{mono} = 1000/3 \text{ px} \quad (\text{line-pairs/mm}) \tag{5.2}$$

and, for a colour CCD imager,

$$r_{colour} = 3 \text{ px} \sqrt{3} \quad (\mu m) \tag{5.3}$$

and

$$R_{colour} = 1000/(3 \text{ px } \sqrt{3}) \quad \text{(line-pairs/mm)} \qquad (5.4)$$

For the M-5 chip, with 9.2 μm square pixels, monochrome resolution is 36 LP/mm, from which we calculate the colour resolution to be 36/1.73, or 21 LP/mm.

It is obvious that colour quality from spatial multiplexing can only be as good as the interpolation algorithm used to gather data from surrounding photosites. Most manufacturers have their own proprietary algorithms which typically take a 3 × 3, or 5 × 5 matrix around each pixel. Whereas the DN (digital number) value of the colour band sensed by the photosite in question is assigned directly from the received signal, the other two colours required to create the RGB image are derived from the surrounding 8 pixels (3 × 3 matrix), or 24 pixels (5 × 5 matrix).

Spatial multiplex systems are not without their disadvantages, however, the main problem being that because of the averaging or resampling of pixel intensities, artifacts can occur in the image of an object that has sharp edges or strong lines. Known as *aliasing* such artifacts manifest themselves as stair-stepped jagged edges, particularly when the display or printed resolution is too coarse to hide the effect. However, a suitable anti-aliasing technique known as *dithering* exists for printing. By this process the edges of an image can be softened to remove the worst aliasing effects.

Although it is possible to derive monochrome images from colour simply by averaging the RGB bands, it is not a recommended practice since this leads to double averaging and reduced discrimination in the image.[29] It should be remembered that a colour interpolation algorithm already does an averaging job, effectively acting as a smoothing filter across the image.[30] Nevertheless, it is easy to produce a monochrome print from a colour image simply by selecting the grey-scale option in the printing commands, or by selecting a mono-channel from Photoshop's Channel Palette (see Chapter 6).

For the DCS-200, the colour image follows the same style route as its monochromatic counterpart, but now there are three channels of data to accommodate. As shown in Fig. 5.6, each RGB data stream will go to the A/D converter (ADC), and then to the DSP (without compression however) where contrast and detail are adjusted before storage in the hard disk.

In the case of the latest DCS cameras (where image compression takes place) the DSP uses its own special algorithm, known as *run adaptive differential compression* (RADC). Kodak use this proprietary compression instead of JPEG or other standard compression algorithms because RADC allows the camera to store more high-quality images. Compression with JPEG starts with a full resolution colour image, but it's more efficient to start with pixel values coming directly from the CCD chip because they contain only a third of the data of the final colour-image file. Thus for the DCS-420, DCS-410 and the EOS.DCS-5 cameras (which have the same chip as the DCS-200) the 4.5 Mb RGB file is stored in compressed form at around 1.5 Mb on a standard PCMCIA (PC Memory Card International Association) card. In addition, these cameras have frame buffers that hold 12 bits per colour—a total of 36 bits—but from this large capacity only the best 8 bits from each band are selected, leaving the final image capacity at 24 bits of data, as with the earlier DCS-200, but with improved quality.

An important specification for a digital camera is its *pixel depth*, or bit capacity. Pixel depth is set by the number of bit-planes in the frame buffer, and in order to avoid

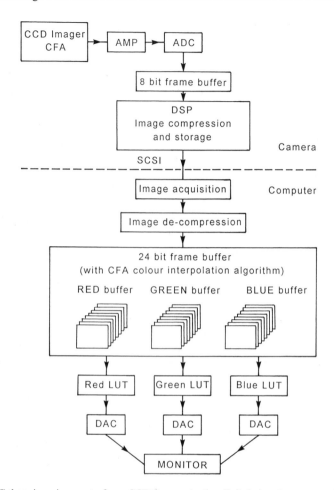

*Fig. 5.6* Colour imaging route from CCD imager to the digital signal processor (DSP), image commpression and computer (via SCSI interface). After the image has been decompressed, colour signals are sent to respective buffers and look-up-tables (LUTs) before digital-to-analogue conversion (DAC) and presentation at the monitor.

*contouring* (when bands of constant intensity between pixels start to appear) it is essential that at least 24 bit colour is available. A pixel depth of 24 bit planes means a possibility of $2^{24}$ (16 777 216) colours.

After going through DSP and storage in the camera's hard disk, the images are then downloaded through an SCSI port to the host computer, where proprietary image acquisition software stores the RGB data in a 24 bit frame buffer for CFA (colour filter array) interpolation.

## *Kodak DC 40: a technical discussion*

The Kodak DC-40 is of interest due to the fact that it has well documented technical data, though no longer in production it did, some years ago, give very reasonable pictures which even today might be considered useful. With only 756 × 504 pixels (0.38 MPx) it has the capability of providing the very minimum of acceptable quality, in monochrome or colour.

For the Kodak DC-40 camera compressed images are stored on 4 Mb of Flash EPROM (erasable programmable read-only memory) built into the camera (the flash memory retains data even if the batteries run down or are removed). The DSP can compress images at two different levels: medium resolution mode with 256 × 384 px (32 : 1 compression) and full resolution mode with 504 × 756 px (16 : 1 compression). The compression mode is selected using Kodak's image acquisition software (PhotoEnhancer) when the camera is connected to the computer.

According to Kodak DC-40 Technical Facts (published via Internet) the three data channels for this camera (and most possibly others as well) are: (i) luminance (based on green wavelengths), (ii) red-green and (iii) blue-green. All of which are compressed and stored on 4 Mb of Flash EPROM which maintains its contents without electrical power, and whose contents can be erased and reprogrammed within the computer.

Each pixel on the CCD is mainly sensitive to only one primary colour of course, either red, green or blue. But the adjacent pixel colour interpolation algorithm is there to make sure that every pixel (despite its designated filter colour) will receive its correct colour identity, according to the image colour at that position in the array.

Kodak CFA interpolation first calculates green values at the red and blue photosites, and then calculates the missing red and blue values at the other photosites. Vertical and horizontal gradients are then calculated to deduce whether the missing green pixel lies along a vertical or horizontal image edge. The missing green value is formed by interpolating the values along the edge. For example, horizontally adjacent green pixel values are used if the missing green pixel is located along a vertically oriented edge. Once the missing green values are interpolated, the missing red and blue values are calculated by linearly interpolating the red-to-green and blue-to-green chrominance ratios. This effectively increases sharpness by adding high frequency luminance details to the red and blue records.

Next, image edges are sharpened with adaptive FIR filters (a computer processing filter used to sharpen edges). Vertical and horizontal high-frequency details are extracted from the green channel and added back to the red, green and blue signals.

Colour correction is then applied to improve colour saturation. This is needed because the filters over the pixels are not perfect, the red photosite having some response to green and blue light, the blue pixel to red and green, and so forth. Fast colour matrixing techniques correct for the unwanted responses to improve colour saturation.

Further image processing can be done by transferring the proprietary camera image file (such as the Kodak KDC file for the DC-40 camera, or other native image files) to any other bit-map file supported by TWAIN compatible software, such as TIFF (tagged image file format) or PCX, or PICT (a native graphics format for Macintosh computers), all standard formats for bit-mapped images (see Box 4).

After being processed and stored in the three (8 bit) frame buffers, the three digital signals are now sent to three *look-up tables* (LUTs) on line between the buffers and the monitor DACs, where real-time colour enhancement takes place. Each LUT is effectively a table of numbers that create an index with pixel values stored in its

---

### Box 4  Bit-mapped images and object oriented graphics

Two terms that appear regularly in digital imaging are *bit-mapped images* and *object oriented graphics.* Although we are mainly concerned with bit-mapped images it is important to understand the difference between the two graphic forms.

A *bit-mapped* image is composed of a series of dots (pixels) rather than a set of lines (or vectors), and consists of a grid of discrete pixels, each with its own grey value or colour. The bit-mapped image is located within a high-speed frame buffer, where each pixel (stored as a binary number) has an $x$, $y$ address that maps to a pixel located in the monitor (CRT) display. Resizing a bit-mapped image without any distortion or aliasing is very difficult, and bit-mapped images consume large amounts of computer memory. Bit-mapped images can be taken from: (a) digital cameras, (b) scanned photographs or (c) digitised (frame-grabbed) video.

*Object oriented* (*vector*) *graphics* allow an image to be defined mathematically, rather than by a set of dots, and are much more economic with storage space. Unlike bit-mapped images, object oriented graphics can reproduce circles or squares without aliasing or distortion, and require much less computer manipulation. For this reason object oriented graphics are mainly used for drawing and CAD (computer aided design) programs.

---

associated buffer. The number of entries in each LUT is being set by the number of bit planes. For 8 bit planes there are 256 entries in the LUT and it is these that are sent to the display—rather than those in the buffer. By using LUT entries it is possible to preserve the original digital values in each frame buffer, while the computer operator is free to manipulate LUT data for real-time image processing with software such as Photoshop. The advantage of the LUT system is that it allows for iterative experiments to be made with the image. For example, if the blue pixels are too strong (say a DN value of 150) they can be reduced to a DN of say 80, without destroying the original (buffer) values. Colour adjustments can be seen immediately and changed or kept accordingly.

From Fig. 5.6 we see that binary image data (the binary digit can be either 0 or 1) is sent to one of three frame buffers according to the pixel colour in the CCD imager's CFA. For a 24 bit colour system each RGB buffer will have 8 bit planes which means 256 ($2^8$) brightness levels for each hue.

The bit-mapped image data are now interpolated in the 24 bit frame buffer, pixel by pixel, so that every pixel will have an appropriate brightness in either red, green or

# The Digital Image

## Key to Colour Section

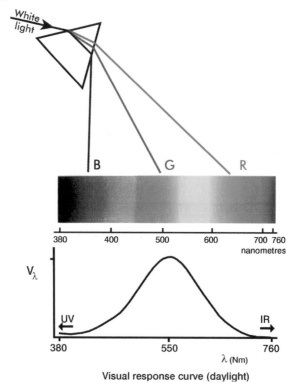

*Fig. 2.10* Prismatic spectrum and $V_\lambda$ curve.

*Fig. 5.5* A Bayer colour filter array.

(a)

(b)

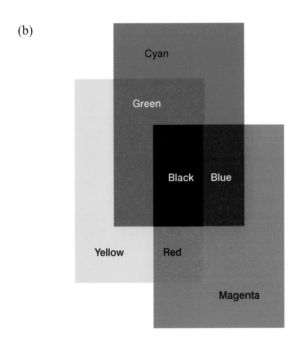

*Fig. 2.11* (a) Additive colour synthesis from the three primary colours: red, green and blue. (b) Subtractive colour synthesis from the three complementary colours: cyan, magenta and yellow.

## IV

*Fig. 3.8* Scanned face (Cannon IX - 4015) of a colour photograph (insert), reproduced with $n = 374$ and $M = 32$ colours. $I_c = 1870$ bits.

(a)

(b)

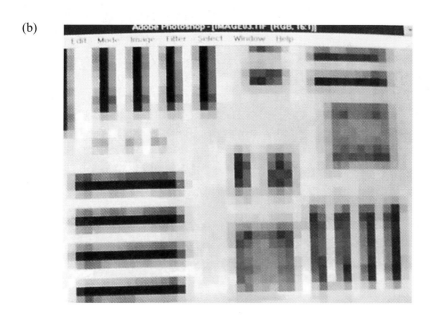

*Fig. 5.7* Resolution and CFA interpolation. (b) Reproduction of the target suffers from CFA interpolation (manifest as an RGB pixel display at the outer edges of each black line) plus Nyquist limitations

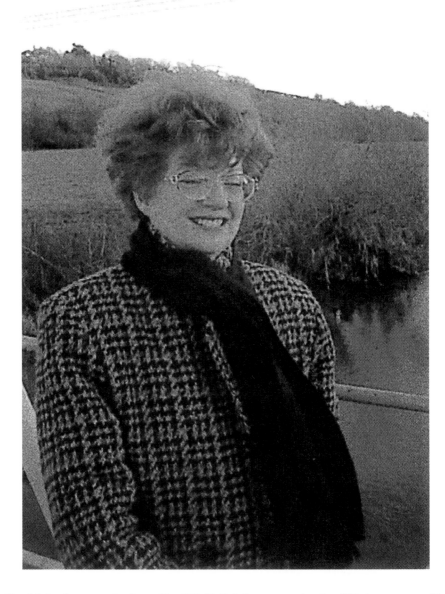

*Fig. 5.9* Outdoor portrait taken with a DC-40 digital camera, printed on HP glossy paper with HP 560C (inkjet) colour printer (Photo: Ron Graham)

(a)

(b)

*Fig. 6.1* Typical example of image enhancement using Photoshop 3.0. (a) Raw TIFF image taken from 1500 feet with DCS-200 camera. (b) Enlarged and enhanced version with: (i) improved colour balance and contrast. (ii) Gaussian blur (to minimise aliasing), (iii) unsharp masking (to gain better definition) and (iv) fine adjustment of brightness (Photos: Ron Graham and Jon Mills). Note: The photograph in (b) has ben 'manipulated' as explained on pages 95 and 96.

*Fig. 5.8* A Kodak DC-40 colour image printed in monochrome.

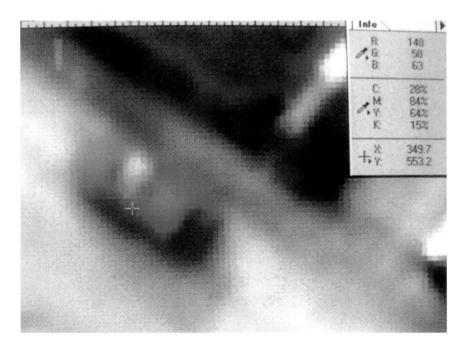

*Fig. 6.3* Photoshop 3.0 *Info* drop-down menu with air photo of road scene.

(a)

(b)

*Fig. 6.5* In Fig. 6.5a the pale sky is made darker in Fig. 6.5b by use of the *Curves* command in PHOTOSHOP 6.

(a)

(b)

*Fig. 6.10* Landscape photograph showing (a) powerline across the sky and (b) powerline removed using image processing tools discussed in Chapter 6.

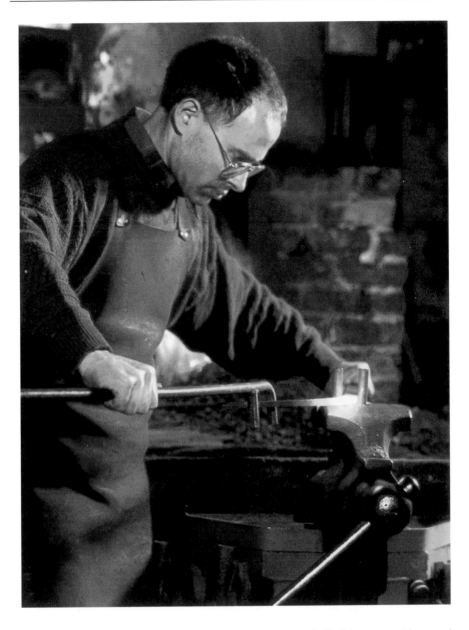

*Fig. 8.1* Forge worker, a Fuji FinePix S2 Pro shot, with electronic flash in support. Photograph by John Bigglestone, of John Bigglestone and Company.

*Fig. 8.2* Studio electronic flash portrait, Fuji FinePix S2 Pro with Nikon 80–200 mm Zoom lens. Photograph by John Bigglestone, of John Bigglestone and Company.

*Fig. 8.3* Advertising shot, Nikon 80–200 mm Zoom lens, Fuji FinePix S2 Pro. Manipulated and enhanced by Photoshop 6. Photograph by John Bigglestone, of John Bigglestone and Company.

*Fig. 8.4* Industrial Panorama of an old engineering workshop before the firm moved to new premises. The six photograph panorama was taken with a Nikon 35–70 mm lens on a Fuji FinePix S2 Pro. The panorama was manipulated in Photoshop 6. Photograph by John Bigglestone, of John Bigglestone and Company.

*Fig. 8.9* Remote Sensing image taken with the Kodak DCS-420 CIR camera. The bright red cluster of plants near the centre of the frame is an illegal plot of cannabis plants. Image courtesy of US Forest Service and Dr W.S. Warner.

*Fig. 8.10* Photograph of Freeport Copper mine in Iryan Jaya (western New Guinea). Taken from helicopter (Bell 412) at an altitude of 18 000 feet, the height of the mine was ca 12 000 feet. The camera was the Kodak DCS-460 CIR and the photograph was taken in the false-colour infrared mode, with a 28 mm lens. Photograph by: Ron Graham and Alexander Koh.

*Fig. 8.12* The pre-planned aerial survey of a coastal mission with the MF-DMC II, (Hasselblad 555 ELD) this map is by courtesy of MapSource, and shows the position of each of the 60% overlapping images. Flying height is 4000 feet above ground, and the lens was a Zeiss Distagon 40 mm (calibrated). The runs were from Lyme Regis to Charmouth in Dorset.

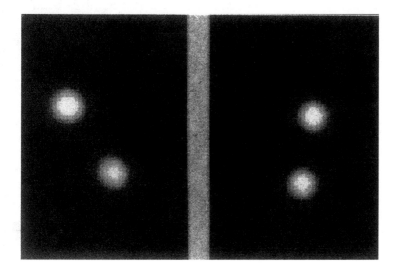

*Fig. 8.16* Binary star Capella recorded in two successive CCD images, and image processed by the COAST system. The two resolved bodied (separated by 55 milliarc seconds) are shown rotating around each other. Images courtesy of J.E. Baldwin, Cavendish Laboratory, Cambridge University, and AstroCam Ltd, Cambridge Science Park.

*Fig. 8.15* Photgraph taken with the MF-DMC II of the Charmouth area, this is photo 411. Photograph taken by Alexander Koh.

blue, up to a theoretical maximum of 256 levels for each colour. After interpolation the binary data are then indexed with their respective LUTs before being sent through their DACs to the three (RGB) electron guns of the monitor.

An indication of CFA interpolation is shown in Fig. 5.7 (see colour section), where a four-bar resolution chart (a) has been recorded with a 24 bit colour imager (Kodak DC-40 camera) via a three diopter close-up lens placed in front of the normal camera lens (one diopter $f = 100$ cm; three diopter $f = 33$ cm). When enlarged 16 times on the monitor screen (Fig. 5.7b; see colour section), the black lines can be seen as an RGB pixel display with only the centre of each line totally black while the white spacings are recorded as pixels of varying colour and intensity. As seen in Fig. 5.7b, digital images have this kind of problem with resolution, as explained by the Nyquist theorem in Chapter 3 (Eq: 3.10).

## *Colour monitor*

Although the bit-mapped image may have a 24 bit capacity, this is not much use if the monitor, or the video graphics card within the computer isn't of similar standard. Monitor resolution is quoted in terms of the number of pixels the screen can display, and also by the VGA (video graphics array) card that supports it. Typically a VGA card will support a monitor that has a resolution of 640 × 480 pixels, with a maximum of 256 colours displayed simultaneously from a palette of 262 144 ($2^{18}$) colours, and because it is an analogue display the VGA can resolve a continuous range of grey-tones, or colours.

A higher-quality display is provided by the SVGA (super VGA) card, which can support at least an 800 × 600 pixel array (or even twice that resolution), with up to 16.7 million colours displayed simultaneously.

The interior screen of the monitor's CRT (cathode ray tube) is coated with three RGB phosphors which are held at a strong anode potential. When struck by the electron stream from each gun, the phosphors glow with an appropriate red, green or blue colour, according to the varying strength of the incident beam. However, before the electron beam strikes the phosphor dots, it travels through what is known as a *shadow mask,* which is metal sheet perforated with tiny holes, located just in front of the phosphors. The role of the shadow mask is to guide the electrons to the correct phosphor colour and to provide a more precise and rounded point that can reach only one specific phosphor, and not a group.

The electron beam scans the screen (from left to right) in a non-interlaced video mode, each image frame being refreshed at a rate of 72 Hz in order to eliminate screen flicker.

The actual colour displayed on the monitor screen is due to the process of additive colour mixing, as explained in Chapter 2 (see Fig. 2.11a). The eight major colours are: black, white, red, green, blue, cyan, magenta and yellow. All of which, with their variations due to hue, saturation and brightness (HSB), are created from the three primaries RGB. The tiny phosphor dots are then confused by the human eye to appear as a resolved point of a given colour.

Printers, which use inks, work on the subtractive principle of colour synthesis (Fig. 2.11b) and RGB data are changed to CMYK before being sent to a printer for hard copies. An additional black ink is also used, since the theoretical addition of

CMY only provides for a rather poor black, consequently we talk of CMYK colour for printing (K is used for black, in order to distinguish it from blue).

As previously mentioned, the above description outlines only one example of an image route for the spatial multiplex type of digital image. It should therefore be treated as no more than a guide since digital technology is constantly on the move, and the division of processing between camera and computer will rarely be disclosed by manufacturers.

Although there is little point in listing the entire range of currently available spatial multiple (type 1) cameras, it *is* worth mentioning some of those cameras that currently represent prices and quality within the range. Starting at the low end, we can expect to see cameras with prices below £50 in 2004, and it will be interesting to see if the balance between price and image quality can provide a satisfactory product.

The cottage shown in Fig. 5.8 (see colour section) is a good example of what can be done by reproducing a DC-40 colour image in monochrome (for economic printing), using the *channel palette* and a little image-processing in Photoshop (see Chapter 6 for details).

Where portraits are concerned there is a noticeable, but none too disturbing, granular effect obvious in enlarged areas of skin-tones. The outdoor portrait shown in Fig. 5.9 (see colour section) is a DC-40 image (20 × 13.5 cm) printed on Hewlett Packard premium glossy paper with an inkjet printer. But, when viewed at the normal distance of 25 cm, this print is not noticeably different from a conventional colour photograph. Taken on a cold December day under flat lighting, the image required increased contrast and some improvements to the colour balance. Additional image processing included a degree of *gaussian blur* to remove some of the aliasing, some of which can still be seen (in the original at least) in the overhead power cables, and some *unsharp masking* to sharpen up image detail. Specifications for the DC-40 are shown in Table 5.2.

### *Kodak DCS-460 CIR digital camera*

Although the DCS-460 looks just like the DCS-420 (its host camera is the same Nikon N90) the CCD area-array chip has four times as many pixels and yields an 18 Mb file. Despite a plea to Kodak to retain or remodel this useful camera, it is unfortunately now out of manufacture. When available, in the year 2000, it was extremely useful in the CIR (Colour InfraRed) mode, although priced in the region of £24 000 the 460 CIR model represented the high end of the Type 1 area-array cameras, which is not too surprising since it incorporates the high-resolution M-6 chip, details of which may be found in Table 4.1 under the Kodak sensor KAF-6301. It has a resolution of over 6 million pixels, in a 2048 × 3072 area array and the sensor size is 18.4 × 27.6 mm, which is four times the area of the DCS series 200, 410 and 420 cameras. It is interesting to note that although the nominal spatial resolution of the DCS-460 is the same as that of the earlier models (each pixel is 9 μm square), the image quality is far superior; it easily matches that of any colour film material when output on a suitable printer, such as the dye-sublimation types. The reason for this superior performance is due to the improved CFA (colour filter array) interpolation algorithm incorporated within the DCS-460.

Table 5.2 Kodak DC-40 digital camera

| | |
|---|---|
| CCD image sensor: | Kodak KAF-400 |
| Pixel size: | 9 μm square |
| Fill factor: | 100% |
| Chip size: | 6.9 mm × 4.6 mm |
| Resolution: | 756 × 504 pixels |
| Colour: | 24 bit |
| Storage: | 4 Mb Flash EPROM (up to 48 photos) |
| Image Compression: | Kodak RADC |
| | Full resolution 756 × 504 px (16:1) |
| | Medium resolution 384 × 256 px (32:1) |
| Colour filter array: | Bayer filter. |
| Camera lens: | 8 mm, f/2.8 to f/16 |
| Exposure: | Auto, with override of ± one stop |
| Focus: | Auto, Four feet to infinity |
| Chip speed: | Equivalent to ISO 80 |
| Shutter speeds: | 1/30 to 1/175 (Automatic) |
| Flash: | On camera. Range up to 8 feet |
| Self-timer: | 10 or 20 seconds |
| Camera controls: | Buttons and LCD |
| Attachments: | Tele and close-up lenses |
| Power supply: | Four AA batteries |
| Weight: | 0.5 kg |
| Hardware recommended: | IBM compatible: 80386 or higher CPU |
| | AppleMac II or higher 6 Mb available RAM |
| Operating system | Windows 3.1 or later, MS-DOS 3.3 or later, |
| recommended: | Apple-Mac 7.1 or later |
| Supplied imaging software: | PhotoEnhancer (by Picture Works) |

Each image (in Kodak proprietary format) is stored in the PCMCIA-ATA card, occupying just over 6 Mb, and during download is extrapolated into a full colour image. The 36 bit colour image (12 bits per RGB colour) is actually used in the form of 24 bits because the best 8 bits of each channel are selected for the final image. This can then be saved as a standard image format, say TIFF, to give an image file of 18.6 Mb. With a 170 Mb PC card the DCS-460 can hold up to 26 high-quality 18 Mb images but for extra capacity a 510 Mb card will enable 85 high-quality images to be stored.

With an ISO rating of 100, the DCS-460 allows the user to shoot pictures with the same confidence as though using colour film of the same speed rating. The only restriction is an image capture rate of 12 seconds in the standard mode, but this may vary depending on the host computer. Nevertheless, a burst rate of two images in 2 seconds is available, with an 8 second pause to store each image. Above all, for the professional photographer, the DCS-460 offers the high quality required with almost immediate access to the image, and once experienced this is a convenience few can turn their back on. The DCS-460 *was* available in the usual Kodak range of 460m (monochrome), 460c (natural colour) and 460 CIR (false-colour infrared), the latter being available on special order only.

Perhaps the most critical test for any small format camera is to produce a suitable image in aerial photography, where resolution and fidelity are of the utmost importance. In this respect the reader is referred to Chapter 8 of this text where photogrammetric and remote sensing applications of DCS-460 imagery are explained and reproduced in both natural colour and false-colour infrared.

It is obvious that high-end digital cameras such as the DCS-460 are too expensive for popular use, but the cost does not stop there. An 18 Mb image file takes a lot of processing and since most images will require something like three to four times as much free RAM as the file size, the computer's RAM and hard disk capacity become highly important.

Typically, a PC will require 2 Mb of RAM for its DOS and a further 6 Mb or more for Windows. In addition, image processing software such as Adobe Photoshop can eat up at least 5 Mb, so we have used quite a lot of RAM even before an image file is opened! A photograph of the DCS-460 is shown in Fig. 5.10.

### *Canon EOS 1DS*

This is a 11.1 MPx camera, spanning the full 24 × 36mm format of the 35 mm SLR camera it is housed in. It features a CMOS sensor and is fully compatible with the full range of Canon EOS lenses. The price is £6999.

*Fig. 5.10* The Kodak DCS-460 CIR Digital Camera, a 6 million pixel (CCD) sensor.

## *Canon EOS D60*

Yet another Canon that uses a CMOS sensor, the EOS D60 costs £2000. It has 6.3 MPx the sensor having 3072 × 2048 Px, and a shutter speed range of 30 to 1/4000 seconds. It is an SLR with interchangeable lenses, focusing is typical for an SLR with through the lens (TTL) focus.

## *Kodak DCS Pro 14N*

The DCS Pro 14N, as shown in Fig. 5.11, is built on a Nikon mount and uses a CMOS sensor of 24 mm × 36 mm format. The price of this camera is only £3500, which is well under half of the cost of the Canon EOS 1DS, with a 14 MPx chip this is a good bargain. There are three raw file resolutions 14 MPx, 6 MPx or 3 MPx, in Kodak's Extended Range Imaging (ERI) JPEG format.

## *Fuji FinePix S2 Pro*

Fuji has done itself proud with this SLR which won the 'camera of the year' award for 2002. It has a 6.3 MPx sensor (CCD) and is housed in a Nikon body that can take interchangeable Nikkor lenses. The prices are reasonable at £2000 when fitted with a 24–85 mm lens, or the standard 28–70 mm lens. Shutter speeds are up to 1/4000 and the sensor size is 3024 × 2016 Px with up to an ISO of 1600.

## *Minolta Dimage 7i*

The Dimage 7i has 4.9 MPx (2560 × 1920 Px) CCD, with automatic focus (AF) in a sleek looking SLR body. A 1/4000 shutter and x7 optical zoom (28–200 mm) lens allows for diverse imaging possibilities. Price is very reasonable at £900.

*Fig. 5.11* The Kodak DCS Pro 14n camera, with full 35 mm frame. The sensor is CMOS with a maximum of 14 MPx.

### Contax N Digital

For the first time a full-frame digital SLR has come on the market, by full-frame we mean the digital sensor has the proportions of a 35 mm camera, i.e. 24 × 36mm. The resolution is 3008 × 2008 Px, CCD with 12 micron pixels, which capture more light and in theory will exhibit less image noise. The camera has interchangeable lenses, TTL metering and an ISO range of 25 to 400. Using the camera on 25 ISO gives superb imagery, the low speed being compensated by the full range of shutter speeds which go from 30 seconds to 1/8000 sec plus bulb. Images are recorded as JPEG with a selection of compression ratios from 1/4, 1/8 and 1/16. Files can be saved as TIFF with a size of around 18 Mb, or as 12 bit raw files of about 9 Mb in size. This is rather like a 35 mm camera to operate and the price reflects this at £6000.

### Fuji FinePix 4700

Fujifilm produced the much trumpeted Super CCD in the year 2000, with 2.4 MPx occupying an octagonal honeycomb pattern. The interpolated resolution is quoted as 3.34 MPx, and the shutter speeds go from 3 to 1/2000 seconds. It has adjustable ISO ratings of 200/400/800 and the images are recorded on SmartMedia cards. The $f$/2.8 lens is a 3.7 digital zoom, and the price was £565.

### Leica Digilux 1

The Digilux 1 camera has 3.76 MPx CCD sensor (2240 × 1680 Px), with SD 64 Mb storage card and an 8 to 1/1000 second shutter. The camera has a large 2.5 inch LCD screen for easy composition, and is priced at £600.

### Kodak DCS Pro Back

The Kodak DCS Pro Back is a camera based on two well-known cameras, the Hasselblad 555 ELD and the Mamiya RZ67 Pro II. The Pro Back therefore is really a back attachment providing a digital facility to these two cameras. It has a 16 MPx ITO (indium tin oxide) sensor (4080 × 4080 Px) generating a 48 Mb file, with two slots for CF or CF+ storage cards. Its ISO rating is 100 and can be powered by tethered a/c or with a portable Quantum Battery 2 pack. The quality of images is superb and being of square format the camera is ideal for aerial survey. It is possible to gain black and white infrared photography from this camera by removing the infrared blocking filter from the chip. The chip size is 37 mm square with the usual (Kodak) sized pixel of 9 micron. The price of this camera (Hasselblad 555 ELD) is £15 000.

### MF-DMC 1

This is another 16 MPx camera hosted by the Hasselblad 555 ELD but fitted with a DICOMED back with 4096 × 4096 Px. The chip size is 63.16 mm square, brought about by the size of the pixels which are 15.4 micron each, and the picture size is 57.15 mm square. The MF-DMC 1 is used for normal colour with a 500BP300 (VIS) filter placed in front of the lens. Alternatively, when employed in its colour infrared (CIR) mode, the VIS filter is replaced by a 650BP300 (minus blue) filter to provide a CIR image. The camera is used for aerial photography and is mainly employed in remote sensing. The price of this camera is close to 50% more than the DCS Pro Back, which is sold by GeoTechnologies at Bath Spa University, the MF-DMC 1 is shown with an 80 mm lens in Fig. 5.12.

### Konica Revio KD-500Z

To complete our list of cameras it is important to include a model that is economic yet substantial in its characteristics, the KD-500z seems to be ideal in every way. Costing only £300 and with a 5 MPx array (2592 $\times$ 1944 Px), an all automatic camera that has a 1 to 1/2000 second shutter and an aperture range of $f/2.8$ to $f/8$ is a good bargain.

## 5.4 Single Exposure, Single area-array, Vertical Colour Photosites (Type 2)

At present there is but one of these types, the Foveon X3, CMOS. But it can be assumed that it will be a future development as the technology progresses.

### Sigma SD 9

The Sigma SD 9 is a CMOS based SLR camera, with 3.5 MPx (2268 $\times$ 1512 pixels) with each pixel having three photosites capable of recording each RGB colour in depth. By avoiding the necessity of colour interpolation with the aid of CFA filters the resolution is therefore three times 3.5 MPx, or 10 MPx. The silicon absorbs blue wavelengths at about 20 nm, green at 200 nm and the red wavelengths at around 500 nm.

*Fig. 5.12* The 16 MPx, MF-DMC 1 camera with a 57.15 mm square format, is a Hasselblad 555 ELD fitted with a DICOMED back.

Shutter speeds are from 30 to 1/6000 seconds, and the price is considerably under £2000. Data transfer is by Firewire and USB (1 : 1), and the RAW image capture is lossless in any of three resolutions. The camera is fully explained in Chapter 4.

## 5.5  Single Exposure, Three Area-array (Parallel Acquisition) Cameras (Type 3)

The basic architecture of Type 3 digital cameras is shown in Fig. 5.1b and, although only few in number at the present time, they might well take a greater share of the market in future years. The concept of a three-way, beam-splitting colour system is not new of course. Indeed the most successful model is Technicolor and, although there are considerable advantages to using parallel acquisition, manufacturers generally seem to prefer Type 1 methods at present.

The obvious advantage of Type 3 systems is freedom from having to use *adjacent pixel colour interpolation* and the reduction of *aliasing* in high-contrast areas of the image. Each chip has its own colour to create an RGB composite file and this means colour quality is improved. The beam-splitting system has to be accommodated however, and if a standard camera is employed the back focal length of its lens has to be increased to take this into account, usually restricting the maximum aperture of the lens.

### *Minolta RD-175 digital camera*

Based on the Minolta Dynax 500 35 mm SLR camera, the RD-175 provides a full colour image file of 5 Mb onto a PCMCIA card. The three chips are 16.5 × 12.4 mm in size, each holding an area-array of 380 000 pixels. Chip filteration is biased to the green, with two green chips and one red and blue. The two green chips are shifted optically from each other, theoretically doubling the resolution in the all important green channel. According to Tinsley[31] the RD-175 employs both colour and size interpolation so that the RGB output file has an overall resolution of 1528 × 1146 pixels, rather than the 380 000 quoted for each chip. This file is then compressed to 1.1 Mb and stored on a removable 131 Mb PCMCIA card, that allows up to 114 images. The effective speed of the chip assembly is quoted as ISO 800.

From Tinsley's account the resolution of the RD-175 shows some softening (due to size interpolation) but contrast, over-exposure and colour performance are much better. Priced at (1997) just under £10 000 (including VAT) the RD-175 comes complete with a 24–85 mm AF Minolta zoom lens.

### *Agfa ActionCam digital camera*

Once again using the Minolta Dynax 500 camera, the Agfa ActionCam generates the same 5 Mb 24 bit colour file as the RD-175 which it resembles. This is a one-shot three CCD imager which uses exactly the same chip as the RD-175 with a 28 to 80 mm *f*/4 lens. Recording time is 2.5 seconds per frame and storage is accomplished with a 130 Mb PCMCIA card. White balance is provided for tungsten, flash, fluorescent and daylight conditions.

The minimum system requirements quoted by Agfa are 16 Mb RAM and a 24 bit VGA, and the interface is by SCSI-2. A 1997 price release quotes £4995 (plus VAT), inclusive of lens, PCMCIA memory hard-disk card, battery, battery charger, Adobe Photoshop LE software and Agfa's FotoLook scanner drivers. Truly a good bargain for a parallel acquisition type camera.

## 5.6 Three Exposure, Single Area-array (Temporal Multiplex) Systems (Type 4)

As shown in Fig. 5.1c, temporal multiplex systems solve their three-colour exposure problem by employing a spinning filter wheel. Such imagers are destined for high-quality studio work not only because of their dynamic nature and lengthy exposure times, but because they are designed to produce high quality colour images of still subjects. Usually these systems are incorporated into special 'camera backs' that replace the conventional film slide used in medium and large (5 × 4 inch) format studio cameras.

### *Leaf DCB II digital camera back*

Leaf Systems Inc. produce a number of digital camera backs (DCBs) that are rapidly becoming very popular with high-quality advertising studios, and the DCB II is an excellent example of a Type 3 digital system. A measure of the DCB II's imaging potential is mirrored in its Macintosh computer requirements, where at least 64 Mb of RAM are required for efficient operation and this needs to be supported by at least 0.5 Gb of hard disk.

The Leaf has a monochromatic 30 mm square CCD chip with an area-array of 2048 × 2048 pixels, and colour is provided by a rotating RGB filter wheel, as shown in Fig. 5.1c. The filters rotate in front of the chip within a space filled with an inert gas in order to prevent condensation when the sensor is cooled to its operating temperature. As mentioned in Chapter 4, thermal noise is always a problem with CCD imagers, and for high-quality reproduction the Leaf DCB is kept at about 0 Centigrade with the aid of a heat exchanger built into the back.

Each of the single, filtered exposures, can be as short as 1/1000 second with subjects illuminated from any conventional studio source, including studio-flash. The sequence of exposures is red, green then blue with a download time that depends upon the computer. For a correctly configured Power Macintosh this should take about 5 seconds per exposure, or 15 seconds overall.[32] The Leaf DCB has a SCSI interface to the Macintosh, but the latter has to be fitted with a SCSI NuBus board.

A number of studio cameras can be, and have been, fitted with a Leaf DCB including the Hasselblad, Mamiya, Fuji GX680 and Sinar large format monorail. Current (1997) prices are in the region of £20 000.

### *Leaf Volare*

The Leaf Volare is a digital camera-back with a 2000 × 3000 actively cooled CCD. The colour multishot capture is ideal for still life images and it has a dynamic range of 12 *f*-stops, generally useful for high class portaiture and landscape.

# 5.7 Scanned Linear Array Systems (Type 5)

Scanned linear array systems have been with us for some time in the form of aerospace imaging sensors. Called push-broom imagers, they generally employ a single linear array of pixels for monochromatic records, and three or more linear arrays for colour or infrared false-colour recording.

## *SPOT Push-broom CCD aerospace imagers*

Designed by the French Space Agency, SPOT was the first earth observation satellite to employ linear CCD sensors. Since 1986 two versions of SPOT have been launched into space where they are engaged in remote sensing of the earth. The satellite completes 14 earth orbits per day at an altitude of 830 km (at the equator) and carries two HRV (*haute resolution visible*) imaging telescopes.

As the satellite sweeps forward in its orbit, the 2.5 m long telescopes receive scattered radiation from the earth which is received by the linear arrays of sensors in the focal plane of the telescopes. The linear arrays have 6000 CCDs per scan line, each pixel being 13 µm square. As each scan line corresponds to a swath of terrain perpendicular to the ground track, and as each pixel covers 10 m of ground, the total swath width is 60 km.

The telescopes are designed to operate in either of two imaging modes in the visible and near infrared portions of the spectrum.

- Mode 1: a monochromatic (Panchromatic) mode intended to provide a high ground resolution of 10 m in the 510–730 nm band.
- Mode 2: a multispectral mode consisting of three narrower spectral bands, each with a ground resolution of 20 m and a swath width of 60 km: band (i) 500–590 nm (green); band (ii) 610–680 nm (red); and band (iii) 790–890 nm (near infrared).

SPOT imagery is transmitted directly to a number of receiving stations on earth, from which an internationally available source of data allows users to obtain either hard copies or computer compatible tapes. Many earth scientists, such as geologists, agriculturists, foresters, town planners and cartographers can obtain a wealth of important, and constantly up-dated, information from SPOT, and image-maps at scales of 1 : 50 000 or even 1 : 25 000 can be made from these data files.

## *Agfa StudioCam*

Aimed at the professional studio operator, the Agfa StudioCam is intended for still life product photography of table-top dimensions. Its chief applications are with direct mail catalogues, product brochures and other rapid turn-around documents. It is a custom-built camera incorporating a 36 bit trilinear CCD sensor capable of capturing a wide dynamic range of colour to afford increased detail in shadow and highlight zones. The system sensitivity is 100 to 400 ISO.

The StudioCam employs one-pass scanning with the aid of a precision stepping motor, and covers a 36 × 29 mm area with an effective 4500 × 3648 pixels, by scanning parallel tricolour CCD linear arrays, each with 3648 pixels and a bit depth of 12 bits per RGB colour. Maximum file size is 24 bit, 50 Mb or 36 bit, 100 Mb (software interpolation is not required). Image capture takes place with scan times in the range of 1/200 to 1/30 second per line, and a total recording time between one and ten minutes.

StudioCam is available for both Macintosh and PC platforms, and the Mac software package includes Agfa FotoLook, a Photoshop scanning plug-in; FotoTune colour matching profiles; FotoFlavor colour enhancement plug-in; Photoshop 3.0 LE and Canto Cumulus archiving software. The package also includes a Nikon 35-80 AF (auto-focus) lens, all for a total price of around £8500 (excluding VAT).

# 5.8 Scanning CCD Backs for Studio Cameras (Type 6)

A description of some of some types of camera back has already been given under Type 3 systems. But here we are concerned with scanned linear arrays such as the so-called *slip-in* digital camera backs.

### *Phase One, PhotoPhase Plus*

Phase One is a Danish company, and was the first to place a slip-in scanning back on the market with the PhotoPhase FC70 back. Designed for use with 5 × 4 inch studio cameras like the Sinar P2, the back is directly connected to the computer. The PhotoPhase scanning software requires no more than 24 Mb of RAM and is designed to produce a 24 bit RGB TIFF file that can be imported into Photoshop.

A pre-scan provides a low-resolution image that allows the operator to check framing and exposure, together with the line-scan speed set which can vary from 1/15 to 1/125 second. Scanning speed depends upon the processor used, with a maximum of around 30 Mb/minute using a 9500 Power Macintosh.

PhotoPhase Plus can be relied upon to produce very high-quality colour images with a good dynamic range. Current price is around £15 000.

### *Dicomed 5 × 4 inch slip-in camera back*

Inserted just like a conventional 5 × 4 inch film slide, the Dicomed uses a Kodak KLI-6003 chip with three (RGB) parallel linear arrays each with 6000 pixels. The scanned resolution is 6000 × 7520 pixels over a 72 × 90 mm area, and the system applies a one-pass colour scanning time determined by exposure and resolution settings. This is a 36 bit system with user selectable image resolution up to 83 pixels/mm, and independent LUTs for real-time 24 bit file storage. In addition, image contrast, colour balance and dynamic range can be optimised for each scan.

The Dicomed scanning back can be used with any 5 × 4 inch camera, with full 'camera-movements' included. There are also optional adaptors for use with the Mamiya RZ67 and RB67 cameras. A typical price for this back is in the region of $22 000 (USA).

### *Leica S1*

The Leica S1, is available in a range of speeds and resolutions. The current Leica S1Pro has a 5140 pixel chip scanning an area 36 mm square, producing 76 Mb file. The scan frequency synchronisation circuit allows the use of standard 50 Hz lighting. The image quality from the tri-linear chip is beyond reproach, and a full range of accessories is available, including a tilt/shift adaptor for use with the Hasselblad medium format lenses.

## 5.9 Single Exposure, Single Area-array Camera Backs (Type 7)

In this concept the single-shot digital camera back represents the best of all worlds for those professional photographers who simply wish to exchange film for CCD as the imaging medium. Just as film has always allowed medium and large format cameras to be employed in a large range of work, including subjects in motion, so is the need for a CCD system to do likewise, without any restrictions such as an on-line computer.

### Kodak DCS-465 multi-format camera back

Fitted with an M-6 CCD chip (Kodak KAF-6301) providing a resolution of 6 million pixels, the DCS-465 camera back can be supplied for 5 × 4 inch or 120 size cameras. It has also been designed for exclusive attachment to a number of professional studio cameras such as the Sinar, Horseman, Mamiya and Hasselblad. In every case the camera can be used as with film, either in the studio or on location. Each image provides 18 Mb of data with 36 bit colour, conveniently stored on PCMCIA-ATA type IV cards (both flash-memory and hard-disk cards).

For location work, power is provided by a nickel-hydride battery sufficient for an hour, and a capacity to shoot 100 images, while in the studio the system can be operated from the a/c mains. Image capture takes 12 seconds from either source, depending on the removable media used. If a typical 105 Mb PCMCIA card is employed, the operator can store 17 full-resolution (18 Mb) images, and cards with larger capacities are always available. A useful extra is the built-in voice recording which can be made directly onto the storage disk using the DCS-465 incorporated microphone.

Although the uncompressed file size is 18 Mb, compression to 6 Mb is used when images are sent to the PCMCIA disk. When used in the studio, however, images may be downloaded directly to the computer. Prices vary of course, depending on the camera. But it is reasonable to expect a typical Sinar or Horseman DCS-465 to be in the region of £25 000, or more.

### Sinar Sinarback 54

The Sinarback 54, has a Kodak KAF-22000CE chip of 22 MPx, and was developed by Kodak specifically for Sinar. It has a 4080 × 5440 pixel array with 9 μm square pixels, and has a capture rate of one shot every six seconds. It is priced at around £21 300.

## 5.10 Future Developments

Although digital camera developments are fast (and almost impossible to predict) there are some indications that a new class of image sensors, known as complementary metal oxide semiconductors (CMOS), will be strong competitors to CCD within a year or two. Their main advantage is economy, since they are cheaper to manufacture, and they also tend to have fewer defects. Unlike CCDs, which must transfer their charge through neighbouring pixels, each CMOS pixel has its own amplifier and output, which means it can be read out independently and so permit variable frame-rates.

Another development utilises conventional CCDs, but employs optical *diffraction* (see Chapter 1) to increase apparent resolution by a factor of four. The Japanese Pixera Corporation has invented a method where low-priced, medium-resolution CCD arrays, can be turned into high-resolution devices by shifting a single pixel element onto four different areas of a CCD sensor. Evidently this technology can be employed with CCD *and* CMOS systems and, again, the main thrust is in producing better image quality at much less cost to the consumer. From what is known, all Pixera products rely heavily on software since raw pixel data go direct to the computer for image processing.

# 6   Image Processing

If, for a moment, we ignore built-in system processes such as image compression and adjacent pixel colour interpolation, we could say that most of the widely used image processes fall into four distinct categories: *enhancement, manipulation, transformation* and *analytical processing*. All but the last of these processes are as common to conventional photography as they are to digital imaging, although the first three are generally known as 'after treatment' or 'darkroom techniques' and are of course much slower! The exception, analytical processing, adds a further dimension to image processing in that it allows the operator to employ proprietary software to analyse image data, and even supplement this by interfacing his/her own programming to the installed software. Image files such as BMP, TIFF etc., may then be analysed to provide data for scientific, industrial, commercial or social research.

## 6.1   Practical Applications of Image Processing

*Image enhancement* means improving the quality of an image; *manipulation* is concerned with making changes to its content while *transformation* takes care of any required geometric and dynamic changes.

On the other hand, *analytical processing* evaluates spatial and radiometric image components, which are then put to algorithms specially computed to provide either programmed solutions, or to discriminate or emphasise various aspects of the image in terms of tone or colour.

It is generally accepted that image processing increases an image file considerably, and in order to have a comfortable margin the computer should have a RAM capacity at least four times the expected image file size. Currently I have 200 Mb of RAM but, like many others, I find this should be improved by a factor of two at least, if only to speed up operations let alone accommodate an ever increasing number of files and programs.

### *Image enhancement*

The most common enhancement procedures are: *contrast and brightness control, colour balance and correction* and the use of filter algorithms to provide *image blur and anti-aliasing, despeckle,* and *dust and scratches removal.* These are a few of the facilities incorporated in high-quality software such as Micrografx Picture Publisher, Apple PhotoFlash, and of course current and future versions of Photoshop.

Before any form of image processing it is always good practice to inspect the *histogram* for any given image. Regardless of the software employed, all histograms exhibit the same kind of display; a simple distribution of vertical lines arranged across a horizontal axis that represents dark tones at the left, through mid-tones in the centre, to highlights at the right of the diagram. The histogram shows the tonal distribution of an image (grey tone or colour) and helps to determine how these values can be adjusted to improve quality. Usually a good image will have a well-distributed display, with most of the pixels occupying the mid-tones and with less at the shadow and highlight ends. Typically, a low-key image will show most of the pixels crowding the left-hand side of the histogram, whereas a high-key image will tend to crowd the right-hand side of the histogram display.

The histogram palette is also a very useful guide for indicating the contrast of an image. As we know, a low-contrast image appears grey, with hardly any shadows or highlights. In this case the histogram will be crowded in the centre, with few or no pixels at either end. On the other hand, a high-contrast image will have few mid-tones and most of the pixels will be at each end of the display.

Digital enhancement has already been mentioned in Chapter 5 where, for example, Fig. 5.8 is an original colour image enhanced and printed in monochrome (by using the green-channel palette option in Photoshop) to create a grey-scale image for printing. In Fig. 5.9, where we have a DC-40 outdoor portrait which (after transfer from its native KDC file to TIFF) has been enhanced with improved colour balance and contrast, some Gausssian blur (to remove aliasing) and some unsharp masking to provide sharper image detail. These enhancements are done routinely with digital images, mainly because of the character of the medium, but also because it is a simple procedure that can be accomplished on the computer screen much more efficiently than with traditional darkroom printing techniques.

More obvious enhancement is illustrated in Fig. 6.1 (see colour section), where the typically flat appearance of the aerial photograph shows little contrast (because of haze) and poor colour discrimination. Recorded in the evening at 1500 feet with a DCS-200 camera, the raw (TIFF) image shown in Fig. 6.1a has had no further treatment.

Image processing in Photoshop has made a considerable difference, as shown in Fig. 6.1b, and if we ignore the obvious manipulations, we can list the enhancements made to Fig. 6.1a, as follows:

## Improved colour balance and contrast

These improvements are made from the *IMAGE* menu found on the Adobe Photoshop screen header. Using the left-hand mouse button the operator can click-on (c/o) this menu to view a pull-down list of functions, from which a (c/o) *Adjust* leads to yet another list, and then (c/o) *Auto Levels* automatically finds the best colour balance and contrast (clips the histogram at the black and white points ±5%).

## Gaussian Blur

Found under the *FILTER* menu, *Blur* is selected and then (from the following menu) *Gaussian Blur*. Although the term has statistical connotations (a normal distribution of pixels), in practical terms the process feathers the edges of an image to minimise the effects of aliasing. Control of Gaussian blur is accomplished by selecting the pixel radius, in this case 0.5 pixels.

### Unsharp Mask

Found once again under the *FILTER* menu, we first (c/o) *Sharpen,* then (c/o) *Unsharp Mask* in the following drop-down menu. Here we find three controls: *Amount*, *Radius* and *Threshold,* and in Fig. 6.1b, these were given the values 150%, 1.6 Px, and eight levels, respectively.

Unsharp masking was first undertaken with conventional photographic processing by making an unsharp diapositive contact print (of low contrast), and then registering this with the negative to provide a new negative of lower density range. Not only did this provide a density range that could be printed onto a contrasty grade of paper, but because the fine detail in the diapositive was lost (due to the unsharp positive image) the fine detail in the negative was retained to yield a sharper final image. This process is an excellent method for gaining better image definition, and in some places is still used in aerial photography laboratories, but is very time consuming. What can take a few hours by traditional methods takes only a few seconds on the computer!

### Fine adjustment to brightness

From the *IMAGE* menu *Adjust* is selected then *Brightness/Contrast*, where a slider is moved (with the mouse) until the image looks suitably brighter. In this case an extra 28% of brightness was added to the image.

## Manipulation

Image manipulation takes much more skill than enhancement procedures, neverthe-less it can easily be learnt and the process is great fun! Unlike darkroom manipula-tions, digital work can be accomplished in more comfortable surrounds and with greater efficiency and subsequent quality than with traditional methods. But most importantly, on-screen manipulations are far quicker, and the operator's handiwork is immediately evident at each iterative improvement.

In Photoshop for example, most manipulations are undertaken with a number of *tools* found in the Toolbox column. For the obvious changes shown in Fig. 6.1b, five tools were employed.

As may be seen from Fig. 6.1b, the image has been enlarged and cropped and, apart from obvious enhancement, the four cars parked down the road have been removed, and one of them relocated to crash into a larger vehicle that has backed out of its drive.

It might seem that some artistic ability is required to accomplish such modifica-tions. But the reader has no reason to be concerned since I, who am quite clumsy in this respect, managed reasonably well with hardly any practice!

The manipulation procedure was as follows:

### Enlarging the image

To make the retouching tasks easier it is necessary to enlarge the screen image, and this is done by (c/o) the *WINDOW* menu, then (c/o) *Zoom-in* and selecting a 1 : 2 enlargement.

### Image rotation

This is a transformation function and can be found under the *IMAGE* menu, where three *Rotations* are possible. There are two 90° rotations, *CW* (clockwise) and *CCW* (counter clockwise) and an *Arbitrary Rotation* which allows for any degree in either direction. Image rotation is necessary so that the selected image area to be surrounded by the *Marquee* (see below) can be oriented correctly. For Fig. 6.1a the first vehicle to be moved (by the *Marquee*) required a CW rotation of 60° so that the rectangular *Marquee* could fit closely to the shape of the vehicle.

## Moving image components with the Marquee

The *Marquee* tool can be found at the upper left of the Toolbox and is shown there as a rectangular icon. But it is possible to select an elliptical *Marquee* with a double (c/o) the *Marquee* tool with the mouse cursor. This releases the *Marquee Options Palette* and allows the operator to select the required shape (including squares and circles). To move the rectangular *Marquee* to the subject, in this case the vehicle, all one had to do was (c/o) the tool and drag the *Marquee* over to the vehicle, then surround it as tightly as possible by pressing the mouse button and dragging diagonally from corner to corner. Next all that had to be done was to press the mouse button and drag the enclosed vehicle to the required position. Another (c/o) by the side of the *Marquee* and the vehicle was now relocated and the *Marquee* removed.

A similar procedure was adopted for one of the cars on the road, this time positioning the car to suggest a collision. After which the image was rotated to its correct position once more.

## Pipette, Paintbrush and Pencil

The next task was to wash over the white spaces left by the moved vehicles and remove the remaining three cars on the road. This is a very simple procedure involving the *Pipette* (to sample the correct wash colour from the image), and either the *Paintbrush* or *Pencil* (to either wash over, or wash out the required image area). For larger areas it is convenient to use the *Airbrush* tool but, as the corrections to Fig. 6.1 were small, accuracy demanded smaller tools.

First, the *Pipette* (or *Eyedropper)* was dragged over to the road adjacent to a white space and after (c/o) a suitable area, the mouse cursor was brought back to the Toolbox to (c/o) the *Paintbrush*; the latter was then applied to the white marks (left by the moved vehicles) to cover the road with brush-strokes of an identical colour. The *Pipette* had to be dragged over a number of times in order to match the road colour of course, then by use of *Paintbrush* or *Pencil* the cars were washed out completely. The five tools used in this exercise are shown in Fig. 6.2. These are only five of the twenty available in the Photoshop Toolbox.

## Cropping tool

As may be seen the selected area for cropping is shown by a dotted line within the image space. This was first drawn by (c/o) the *Cropping Tool* with the mouse cursor, then dragging over to the image where the desired cropping was outlined. A further click on the inside of the cropped area and the tool now appears as *Scissors*, indicating that cropping is complete.

## Transformation

Image transformations are generally found under the Photoshop *IMAGE* menu, and include commands such as: *Rotations* (already mentioned above), *Image Size, Flip* and *Effects* commands, with the latter including facilities such as: *Scale, Skew, Perspective*

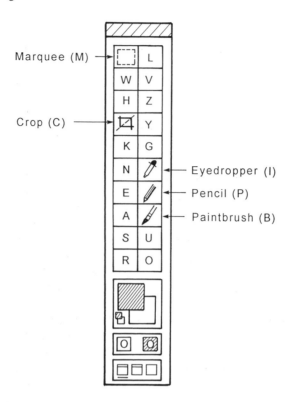

*Fig. 6.2* Photoshop 3.0 Toolbox, showing the five tools emmployed in modifying Fig. 7.1b.

and *Distortion*. These commands allow for geometric changes and, if resizing or rotating for example, will usually require an increase in the number of pixels by the process of *Interpolation*. This does not mean an increase in image resolution, however, but is simply a means to an end. Interpolation in Photoshop is discussed below.

### Resize the image

The *Image Size* command is found under the *IMAGE* menu, and in Fig. 6.1b the image was resized to a width of 6.5 inches. This command was then directed to the inkjet printer, where Fig. 6.1(a, b) was printed on HP Glossy paper.

### Interpolation

Photoshop has three interpolation modes that can be pre-selected by the operator. It is through interpolation that Photoshop determines the DN (digital number) value of pixels to be added or depleted whenever an image is resized or rotated, or given any of the other transformation commands. Photoshop offers the following modes: *Nearest Neighbour*, which is the fastest but lowest quality mode; *Bilinear*, which offers medium quality and speed, and *Bicubic* which is of the highest quality, but also the slowest mode. Bicubic is also the default mode and the one employed for the digital images shown here. All three interpolation modes can be selected from *Preferences* found under the *FILE* menu.

## *Analytical processing*

Although analytical processing suggests some kind of mathematical or computerised process, it must not be forgotten that subjective methods remain the most common, and in many respects the most valuable when in the hands of experienced image interpreters. Those of us with experience in either military air-reconnaissance, air-mapping, or remote sensing readily appreciate the simplicity of the Mark I eyeball, but as satellite imagery and digitised aerial photographs are now common forms of aerospace imagery, analytical processing by computer is a logical addition to conventional methods.

Analytical photogrammetry has been with us for many years now, and similarly computer analysis of satellite imagery for remote sensing has progressed ever since Landsat data were available in the early seventies. Today, there are a number of software programs dedicated to the analysis of aerospace imagery, most of them designed for desk-top image stations. Among these we have software such as: R-Wel Desktop Mapping System (photogrammetry); Meridian Image (image analysis for resource mapping), Arc-Info and Arc-View (cartography); ERDAS IMAGINE (Geographic Information Systems, GIS; and military reconnaissance); and AeroSys Version 2.0 for Windows (photogrammetry).

A typical example of such software is the R-CHIPS system produced by IS Ltd, who sell a 'basic user system' for £5000. R-CHIPS can be installed in any PC 486 machine and upwards with a recommended 120 Mb hard disk capacity. The software includes such items as: histogram equalisation, automatic contrast stretch, overlay operations, density slice images, image statistics, plot profiles, image mathematics, file classifications, image transforms, image registrations and many other functions.

Notwithstanding the high cababilities of these dedicated systems, our old friend Photoshop has a number of useful functions that allow it to be used for processing air-mapping imagery, as will be explained further in Chapter 8.

Astronomical records are usually made with CCD cameras today and, as can be expected, the subject has its share of analytical software. AstroCam software provides for customised image analysis, not only for astronomy, but also for a wide range of scientific applications backed up by a family of CCD imaging systems in support of microscopy and spectroscopy.

Hamamatsu offer the Argus-20 image processor to provide quantitative analysis via a chilled three-chip CCD camera. This system is mainly devoted to microscopy.

Logical Vision Ltd market the WiT software which allows for custom user interfaces, with over 150 different processing functions, and the user can interface with either C programming language, or Visual Basic.

For industry, medicine and research, PC Image is a Windows program for image analysis and processing, with a wide range of tools to count and measure objects, enhance image quality and analyse and display data.

## 6.2 Image Analysis with Photoshop 3.0 and 6.0

Photoshop incorporates some useful analytical functions which can be found under various menus. These commands not only provide a means for measuring the *x, y* location of an image point, but can also show histograms, monochromatic and colour channels, photometric data, and the characteristic curves of images, which can then be adjusted either in full colour or independently for any single red, green or blue channel.

## Rulers

To reveal the *Rulers* dialog box (c/o) the *WINDOW* menu, then *Rulers*. The rulers come as strips along the top and side of the image and can be ruled in various units selected from the *Preferences* sub-menu, found under *FILE*. Once in *Preferences* it is possible to (c/o) *Units* and select any of the following rulers: *Pixels, Inches, Centimeters, Points* and *Picas*.

If *Rulers* is selected with *Pixels,* the entire resolution of the camera (DCS-420) is exhibited with rulers reading from zero to 1524 horizontally, and from zero to 1012 vertically.

## Info

The *Info* box can be brought on screen by (c/o) the *WINDOW* menu, then (c/o) *Palettes* and *Show Info* (for Windows 3.0), and directly under the *WINDOW* menu in Windows 6.0. At this command the *Info* box appears. If the mouse cursor is placed upon a certain point in the image then the info box will display the photometric data and the $(x, y)$ image coordinates of that pixel (in units selected under *Rulers*). The top panel of the info box is designated RGB, and gives the Digital Number (DN) of the colour concerned (up to a maximum of 255), below this is the *percentage* reflection of the image (at the cursor) for CMY, and K with white as zero and black as 100%. By (c/o) the *pipette* alongside RGB we get another menu where we can see the HSB (hue, saturation and brightness) of a given colour under the cursor, then in the bottom panel we find the $(x, y)$ image coordinates.

## Channels

The *Channels* command is useful since it allows the operator to display, and analyse independently, each of the red, green and blue channels that make up the full-colour image. *Channels* can be splayed by first (c/o) *WINDOW*, then *Palettes,* then (c/o) *Show Channels.*

## An example

In Fig. 6.3 (see colour section) we have a raw (air photo) image taken with a DCS-200 camera. This is the same image as that shown in Fig. 6.1a, except that the screen image has been 'zoomed-in' to a scale of 6 : 1. The *Rulers* has been selected with *Points* to gain the highest accuracy. Inspection of Fig. 6.3 reveals a pixelated image of a red car with the cursor (a cross) located on the drivers windscreen. If we now look at the top of the *Info* box we see the following values (in Digital Numbers DN):

$$K = 15\%; R = 148, G = 58, B = 63 \text{ (DN), and the coordinates}$$
$$\text{are } x = 349.7, y = 553.2.$$

An analysis of these values provides the operator with information concerning reflectance and metrication. Before we go on, it will pay us to study these figures more closely. If we put the cursor on the white square below the *Info* box in Fig. 6.3 we get R = 255, G = 255 and B = 255, the maximum possible from an 8 bit system, meaning pure white. The Cyan, Magenta and Yellow reads 0% in each case, as does the value of K (black). But if we place the cursor on a very dark area (just left of the *Info* box in Fig. 6.3) we find the data reads R = 7, G = 19 and B = 33, with the complementary colours C = 74%, M = 54% and Y = 36%, and the value for K = 87%. Which tells us that a pure black would give us a value for K = 100%.

## Reflectance

The reflection factor K is given as 15% black, but in photometric terms a value of 100% is reserved for a perfect white. Therefore we translate K to mean an overall reflectance value of 85% ($\rho = 0.85$), and from this we can calculate the reflection density ($D_p$) according to Eq: 6.1 (see Box 2 in Chapter 2), where:

$$D_p = Log_{10}(1/\rho) \hspace{2cm} (6.1)$$

Obviously, the *Info* box doubles as an on-screen densitometer, and if we substitute 0.85 for $\rho$ in Eq: 6. 1, we get a reflection density of 0.07.

## Colour

By clicking-on the RGB pipette we get a drop-down menu that allows us to select HSB, which reveals values of H = 349°, S = 63% and B = 57%. These values give us a complete analysis for the colour at the image point under inspection. At 349° the hue is a good red (as shown by the colour wheel in Fig. 6.4), with a saturation of 63% and brightness of 57%.

## Metrication

The selected image point shown in Fig. 6.3, has coordinates x = 349.7, y = 553.2, and, although individual pixels may not be too obvious here, they are perfectly visible in

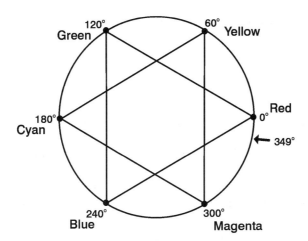

*Fig. 6.4* Photoshop 3.0 colour wheel, showing hue position (349°) of the car bonnet in Fig. 7.4.

the original print. As a consequence, it is possible to measure any point in the image with considerable accuracy, and with known ground measurements (ground truth) scale subjects within the frame.

## Curves

The *Curves* command provides a useful graph which allows the operator to adjust input-to-output relationships for any given area of the reproduction. Intuitively one can adjust shadow, mid-tone or highlight areas by dragging any point of the curve with the cursor. The output can be viewed immediately and changed if not considered suitable. The *Curves* dialog box can be gained from *IMAGE,* then (c/o) *Adjust* and *Curves,* to reveal the drop-down box shown in Fig. 6.5 (a, b) (see colour section). In Fig. 6.5a we have the picture of a house, but a rather pale sky, its RGB curve is a straight line at 45° which indicates the image has not been altered. By dragging the curve downwards (in the highlight area) we get a much darker result, as shown in Fig. 6.5b, and to save this image all one needs to do is (c/o) OK.

Further analysis of an RGB image can be done by (c/o) the *Channel* panel at the top of the box, to reveal another menu which allows one to sample either the red or green or blue component of the RGB image. In this fashion it is possible to adjust and view a particular channel by (c/o) the *Preview* symbol. By (c/o) any part of a curve we get an *Input/Output* analysis (in terms of pixel brightness), which is displayed just below the curve. A number of sampled points are shown on the curve of Fig. 6.5b, and the *Input/Output* data for one of these points are displayed at the bottom of the box.

# 6.3 Spatial Filtering

Image processing is controlled by software and, as we have seen, is accomplished by resampling the digital number (DN) ascribed to various pixels, either by interpolation or by filtering in the spatial domain. A number of different resampling methods can be used to assign the appropriate output DN and, as we know, three forms of convolution (*Nearest Neighbour Bilinear* and *Bicubic*) are available for the task. Spatial filters are also employed, mainly for improving edge-definition, increasing sharpness and noise reduction.

As we have seen, standard software such as Photoshop includes a number of filters for image processing, but these offer only a fraction of the possibilities available from software devoted to scientific analysis. These programs usually allow the user to apply mathematical inputs that will enable them to improve or extract certain image features.

## *Principles of spatial filtering*

Digital image processing is facilitated by the quantisation of pixels into a binary scale (see Appendix A), usually to a capacity of 8 bits, that is, with image brightness levels (grey scale or colours) on a scale of 0 to 255.

Quantisation, from input to output, allows the image to be modified, improved and compressed, and spatial filtering is one of the mathematical processes for achieving these ends. Known as *local neighbourhood processing,* this particular transformation depends not only on the DN value of the pixel being processed, but also on the DN values of the pixels in its immediate neighbourhood.

Filter

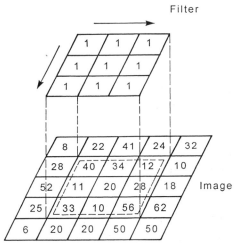

*Fig. 6.6* Spatial filtering. A standard 3 × 3 matrix (kernal) moves over the entire pixel array to modify the image digital numbers (DNs). This kernal acts as a *smoothing* or *low-pass* filter, useful for reducing image noise and speckle.

Spatial filtering uses a technique where a filter matrix *(kernal)* is employed as an operator to produce a convolution with an array of DNs in the image. These *operators* are known as *filters* and they can be in a 3 × 3 matrix, 5 × 5, 7 × 7 or any other odd number geometric array. The standard matrix is 3 × 3 as shown in Fig. 6.6.

There are many different types of filters, each one designed for a specific process, but the most common ones are those used for *sharpening, smoothing (noise reduction), and edge enhancement.* In operation the filter starts at the top left corner of the image and processes a 3 × 3 *window* of that portion of the image according to values within the *kernal.* The objective is to change the central pixel within the 3 × 3 window.

## Smoothing filter: an example

In Fig. 6.6, the kernal represents an averaging (smoothing) filter which, starting from the top left of the image, will operate on the nine image elements shown in Fig. 6.7a, in accordance with Eq: 6.2.

$$g(x, y) = 1/M \sum f(i, j) \qquad (6.2)$$

where:

    *i* and *j* are the respective rows and columns in the image window,
    *M* is the product of *i* and *j*.

Taking each row of pixels in the window we have the sum and average of the convolutions, as:

$$\sum(8 \times 1) + (22 \times 1) + (41 \times 1) \qquad = \qquad 71$$
$$\sum(28 \times 1) + (40 \times 1) + (34 \times 1) \qquad = \qquad 102$$
$$\sum(52 \times 1) + (11 \times 1) + (20 \times 1) \qquad = \qquad \underline{83}$$
$$\sum f(i, j) \qquad = \qquad 256$$

$$g(x, y) = 256/9 = 28$$

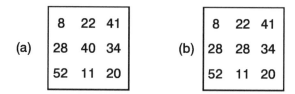

(a)
```
8   22  41
28  40  34
52  11  20
```

(b)
```
8   22  41
28  28  34
52  11  20
```

(c)
```
28  26  24
28  27  28
22  28  35
```

*Fig. 6.7* The effects of low-pass filter shown in Fig. 6.6 (a) Original pixel values (top left 3 × 3 array of Fig. 6.6. (b) After smoothing the 3 × 3 array in (a) is changed, with the centre pixel now DN = 28. (c) After smoothing *all* pixels in (a), we have a completely new set of pixel values, with a lower dispersion of DNs.

As a consequence, the centre pixel shown in Fig. 6.7a has now changed its DN from 40 to 28, as shown in Fig. 6.7b. Naturally the process does not stop there! It moves on to the right, and downwards, pixel by pixel, until every DN in the image has been averaged. For the centre 3 × 3 image window shown in Fig. 6.6 this smoothing operation results in a new window of DNs as shown by Fig. 6.7c.

By comparing the DNs of Fig. 6.6 with those of Fig. 6.7c, it is obvious that the filter has smoothed out the original image DN values to a large extent.

Smoothing, or *low-pass,* filters are generally used for the smoothing out of over-enlarged images, and for removing noise and speckle. In contrast we employ *high-pass* filters for sharpening or edge enhancement purposes, a well-known and much used example being the *Laplacian filter.*

### *Laplacian filter: an example*

Using the same image input as before, the *Laplacian* kernal shown in Fig. 6.8, is operating on the same window as that shown in Fig. 6.6, but this time the effect is quite different.

In a fashion similar to that following Eq: 6.2, the Laplacian operator takes the sum of the DNs in each of the three rows shown in Fig. 6.7a, but instead of averaging it divides the total by 8 to obtain the centre pixel value, as:

$$\Sigma(8 \times -1) + (22 \times -1) + (41 \times -1) \quad = \quad -71$$
$$\Sigma(28 \times -1) + (40 \times 8) + (34 \times -1) \quad = \quad 258$$
$$\Sigma(52 \times -1) + (11 \times -1) + (20 \times -1) \quad = \quad \underline{-83}$$
$$\Sigma f(i,j) = \quad 104$$
$$g(x, y) = 104/8 = 13$$

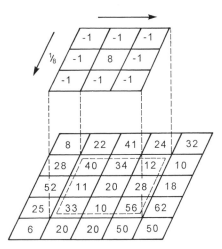

*Fig. 6.8* Laplacian Operator. This kernal produces greater image contrast, and edge-enhancement.

The centre pixel of Fig. 6.7a, is now replaced by the new DN of 13, as shown in Fig. 6.9a. By convoluting the entire centre window of Fig. 6.6 with the Laplacian kernal, we have the completely new pixel array of Fig. 6.9b.

If we compare the results of the two operators on the same image window, then a statistical analysis of the *smoothed* pixels shown in Fig. 6.7c, reveals a standard deviation from the mean of $\sigma = 3.36$. And for the *Laplacian* $\sigma = 14.96$, which indicates a much sharper contrast between the adjacent pixels of Fig. 6.9b, compared with those of the smoothing filter.

Laplacian edge-enhancements are not the only ones available however; others include *gradient* filters and *shift and difference* filters but, whereas these are directional in nature, *Laplacian* operators reveal edges in all directions.

Obviously image processing is a very complex business and, although only touched upon in this text, further information can always be found in the software manuals devoted to scientific data processing and in various papers and textbooks, particularly those dealing with remote sensing.[33][34][35]

*Fig. 6.9* Laplacian Operator. (a) Original DNs shown in Fig. 6.7a, now have a new centre DN = 13. (b) By convoluting the entire centre window of Fig. 6.8 with the Laplacian kernal, we have a new *edge-enhanced* pixel array.

# 6.4 Image File Formats

A *file format* is a structure which defines how information is stored in the file, and how that information is displayed on the monitor or printer. There are a number of graphics file formats available but not all of them can be used universally. With some programs only a specific format can be employed whereas with others, such as Photoshop, a large variety can be used.

Typical of the many well-known file formats that can be used on either Macintosh or PC platforms are: TIFF (tagged image file format), BMP (Windows compatible bit-mapped graphic image), DIB (device-independent bit-map), PICT (Mac supported), EPS (encapsulated PostScript), Photoshop and JPEG.

Possibly the most well-known format, TIFF, was jointly developed by Aldus and Microsoft in 1986 and in its many versions is a standard file format for bit-mapped graphics images. The TIFF standard also defines *data compression* techniques and provides for monochrome and colour images. The TIFF is readily supported by Macintosh, PC/Windows and many other platforms.

Developed by Microsoft, the BMP format was designed to be used under DOS, Windows, Windows NT and OS/2, and can save both monochrome and colour images up to 24 bit. The bit-map DIB format was introduced as a refinement to BMP, and today all Windows and OS/2 BMP files are assumed to be in DIB.

PICT is a general-purpose format supported by Macintosh and used for storing either *bit-mapped* or *object-oriented* images (see Box 4, Chapter 5). PICT bit-maps can provide for grey scale, monochrome or colour with up to 32 bits per pixel (at 32 bits per pixel JPEG compression options are available). PICT format can be saved, opened, or imported by most Macintosh programs and also in some Windows applications, including Photoshop.

EPS is the file format of the PostScript page description language, and is device independent, which means that images can readily be transferred from one application to another. However, an EPS file can only be printed on a PostScript compatible laser printer. EPS can store either bit-mapped or object-oriented images. Using this format one can place images into programs such as Adobe PageMaker, CorelDRAW and Adobe Illustrator, which is why EPS is a popular format for exporting grey scale and colour images to page layout and illustration programs.

Photoshop file format is native to Adobe Photoshop in its various versions and, when working in Photoshop 6.0, files can be opened and saved much more quickly than with any other format. It is also the preferred format for moving Photoshop files between Macintosh and Windows platforms. Photoshop supports JPEG compression in several ways.

JPEG (joint photographic expert group) is the name of the committee that developed the file format for storing compressed images. The format is based on the discrete cosine transform (DCT) algorithm which analyses $8 \times 8$, or $16 \times 16$ pixel arrays (cells) within an image (independent of resolution), and performs an averaging of each cell, dramatically decreasing image size. JPEG employs *lossy compression* techniques that result in some loss of original data and is considered as a baseline standard for this type of image compression.

# 6.5 Image Compression

Digital image files are often very large, and typically a good quality colour image (with at least 8 bits per RGB channel) can consume something like 18 to 25 Mb of memory (depending on picture size). As we have seen (Chapter 5), many digital cameras usefully compress their images before downloading them to the host computer.

The basic idea is to compress the number of image bits to a point where the image is still acceptable, and obviously there are degrees of acceptance here. For some images, with large areas of common tone or colour, a compression ratio of perhaps 20, or even 30 to 1, would not be unacceptable since much of the information is redundant! But if the image were filled with fine detail that must be preserved, then the compression limit might well be set at only 2 to 1!

Compression techniques look at the following redundancies as a means of reducing the size of an image file.[36]

- Repetition of data.
- Redundancy in the way the data are coded.
- Redundancy between adjacent pixel values.
- Psycho-visually redundant information.

The first three of the above techniques are *lossless* methods that do not change the original image at all, but the compression ratios are relatively small, usually 2 : 1 or 3 : 1. The fourth method is known as a *lossy compression* and can be as high as 30 : 1. Obviously the amount of compression has to be balanced with desired quality.

The most well-known example of *lossy compression* techniques is JPEG, as mentioned above. Other *lossy* examples are fractal transforms, and Kodak's RADC which allows for compressions of 16 : 1 and 32 : 1 (see Table 5.2) when used with their DC-40 camera.

JPEG was specifically designed to discard information that is not easily perceived by the eye and makes use of known facts concerning human vision. To start with, the sensitivity of the human eye decreases as spatial frequency (of image detail) increases.[37][38][39] Secondly, we can detect small changes in luminance (brightness) more easily than small changes in colour.[36][40] Thirdly, it has been shown that in photographic prints at least, monochromatic detail is best discriminated in the lower mid-tones where $\Delta D_p$ is of the order of 0.03.[39][41] Finally, research with a reference print has shown[39][41] that for a continuous-tone image containing 6 bits of luminance, about 3 bits contain 80% of the total intelligence.

With the aid of a discrete cosine transformation (DCT) the JPEG algorithm removes visually redundant information by quantising image data in the frequency domain. It then converts it back again (*decompression*) with its inverse function (IDCT). For colour images this process is carried out separately for the three RGB channels.

Recent research[36] has identified a number of distortions common to JPEG compression, among them *blocking* (where a block pattern occurs at high compression, caused by the independent processing of pixel blocks), severe degradation of edges, loss of fine detail, and shifts in tone or colour.

As may be expected, compressed or uncompressed image quality is dependent upon viewing conditions as well as the nature of the image itself.

### JPEG image compression with Photoshop

Photoshop automatically decompresses a JPEG file as soon as it is opened, and when *Save* is selected from the *FILE* menu, JPEG is one of the format choices. A dialogue box then allows one to choose an *Image Quality* level: Low, Medium, High or Maximum. If 'maximum' is selected a larger file of higher quality will be produced, and if 'low' is the choice, then a smaller file of lower quality will be provided.

### Lossless compression

A number of software products can compress images using *lossless compression* techniques. Among those suited to the Macintosh are: StuffIt Delux, DiskDoubler, now Utilities and Compact Pro. Each of these can compress Photoshop images as well as other files.

The standard for PC platforms is PKZIP, which is a shareware DOS application published by PKWare. For those who prefer to use Windows rather than DOS, there is WinZip which features PKZIP to compress files and PKUNZIP to decompress archives.

It must always be remembered that lossless compression ratios are much lower than those gained from lossy compression! On the other hand, lossy compression and decompression, as with JPEG for example, is a slow process (depending on the speed of the computer's processor) because of the amount of computation required.

### Wavelet compression

Wavelet compression transforms signals into a sum of small overlapping waves for analysing, storing and transmitting information. This method is mainly used for scientific applications.

## 6.6  Aesthetic Manipulation

We cannot finish this chapter on image processing without mentioning aesthetic considerations, particularly the elimination of image features that spoil the picture. Figure 6.10a (see colour section), is a case in point. The landscape in this picture is spoilt by a power line running across the sky. Using the *cropping tool* in the Toolbox of Fit. 6.2 to take out the power cable, a narrow white line is left. It is then a question of filling-in with a matching sky-blue (dabbing the *paintbrush tool* in the hatched squares at the lower end of the toolbox until the correct blue is found), then using the paintbrush on the narrow white line of the removed power cable, as shown in Fig. 6.10b.

# 7  Digital Printers

Like all image processes it is the final result that counts, and without a good printer even the finest image file cannot produce a good print!

Over the past decade we have witnessed a number of digital printing innovations and now, it is safe to say, decent quality prints can be produced at reasonable cost from even low-end digital cameras, as shown by Fig. 5.9. Quite apart from printing images, the desk-top printer is undoubtably the most useful peripheral one can buy for a computer, but choice is becoming more and more difficult as different types and standards of printer prolificate.

A number of different kinds of printer are available, including that earliest of models, the *dot matrix* which, though generally thought to be out of date, still enjoys a fair market despite the fact that decent *Inkjet* and *Laser* printers can be purchased very cheaply these days.

In general, electronic printing can be put into two main groups: *impact* and *non-impact.* Impact technology creates an image by literally hammering ink dots onto paper and, although still around in the form of Dot Matrix, its popularity has waned due to poor colour handling, low resolution, low speed and noisy operation. On the other hand, non-impact printing has developed extremely well since 1991 and has managed to overcome all the problems associated with impact types. Other than photographic printing, non-impact methods include *liquid ink, electrostatic, direct thermal,* and *thermal transfer.* Current technology favours non-impact printing and, apart from direct thermal (which is generally reserved for calculators, since image quality is poor and tends to fade), all of the non-impact methods are to be found among the popular digital printers of today.

## 7.1  Dot Matrix Printers

The dot matrix impact printer uses columns of small pins and an inked ribbon to create text and images. Although it is mainly used for black and white text, single and even four-colour ribbons are available. Dot matrix printers are available in 9, 18 or 24 pin configurations, but they are not generally recommended for image production because of their poor quality.

## 7.2  Inkjet Printers

The inkjet printer is fitted with an array of tiny nozzles which spray coloured ink droplets onto paper to produce a full colour image. Most of these printers use liquid inks, but some use sticks of solid inks that liquify at the point of imaging. By employing piezo or thermal methods, anything up to 10 000 droplets per second can be applied by each inkjet nozzle.

Inkjet printers (and laser printers) work by printing a fine pattern of dots with a standard of not less than 300 dpi (dots per inch), now often found as high as 2400 × 4800 dpi. Both monochromatic and colour inkjets are available, but since the colour models do both jobs they are the most obvious choice for imaging purposes. Colour printers such as the HP Deskjet 5550 (A4 size) usually employ two separate ink cartridges, a tri-colour (cyan, magenta, yellow) cartridge, and a black one (total price of the printer is £113). Although a composite of CMY should produce black (see Fig. 2.11b in colour section) in practice the printed colour usually comes out as a muddy brown or green, so the black ink (K) is added to provide a good CMYK image.

Inkjet technology has progressed so rapidly in the last few years that it is not possible to see any difference between a good inkjet print and a silver halide version. The inkjet has got so good that regarding quality there is little doubt that it is the best, true the laser printer is still around and it can produce monochromatic and colour prints at a fraction of the running costs of an inkjet. But for the best colour the inkjet is best. The past five years have seen many changes in printing technology; dye sublimation has almost gone, apart from the Canon CP-10 and CP-100 both with 300 × 300 dpi and which use Canon digital cameras for direct printing, they are priced at £130 and £250 respectfully. Other printers have gone too, such as thermal wax transfer, and pictographic printers, leaving inkjets to reign supreme.

The Epson Stylus Photo 830 has six colours, a colour cartridge of the usual CMY plus two half strength magenta and cyan tones, and another cartridge of black. This is a very reasonable little printer at the price of £87. I have the Epson Stylus Photo 870 (A4) myself and cannot complain, it has the same colour cartridge as the 830 but at £250 is faster and more robust, at a print quality setting of 1440 dpi images print at photographic quality.

The basic inkjet system is roughly drawn in Fig. 7.1, where it can be seen that an ink reservoir feeds each nozzle through a heated capillary. As the ink heats up it forms a minute vapour bubble at the end of the nozzle then, when the heat is turned off, the bubble is released as a fine droplet which is squirted onto the paper with high precision. The system works on what is known as *drop on command* technology where, as soon as the droplet is ejected, a vacuum is formed within the capillary that attracts fresh ink to replace the lost droplet. Another method is to employ a piezo electric crystal to the rear of the ink reservoir. When a drop of ink is commanded, an electric current flows through the crystal which then flexes (rather like a loudspeaker cone), to force a drop of ink through the nozzle.

With conventional inkjets the print-head will take about half a second to traverse an A4 sheet of paper (8.31 inches), and with a resolution of 300 dpi this means a possible 2450 dots across the page, with the print-head switching on and off about 5000 cycles per second. And since the system is one of *drop on command* the print-head has to respond in 1/5000 second! This is truly a wonderful piece of technology, particularly since each nozzle in the print-head has a diameter approaching that of a human hair, with up to 256 nozzles per system, and a heating/cooling cycle that runs many thousand cycles per second.

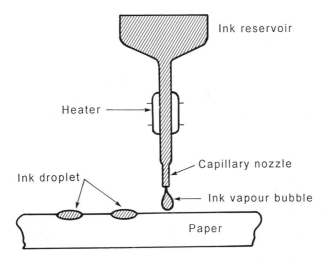

*Fig. 7.1* The basic inkjet system.

I use two thermal inkjet printers: an HP560C (CMYK) inkjet (A4), and an Epson Stylus Photo 870, and have never had a single problem with either of these printers in over five years of continuous use.

Inkjets are sensitive to paper quality, however, and for optimum image quality (monochrome or colour), coated papers are essential. A number of manufacturers market suitable papers for inkjets, among them: Ilford, who produce Ilfojet; Hewlett Packard, who manufacture the Premium Inkjet Glossy Paper and Transparency Films; and the Swiss-based manufacturer, Folex, who market no less than 17 different polyester films and papers, all with special inkjet receptive coatings that provide good resolution and improved colour saturation.

When inkjets deposit ink onto conventional media the ink dots swell and create prolonged drying times which, if one is not careful, lead to smudged prints. Folex, however, manufacture a special microporous coating on their products which draws ink into the surface of the media by capillary action, to facilitate an instant drying and smudge-resistant bonding. The Wiggins Teape PlusJet paper also gives excellent results at a very economic price.

Hewlett Packard offer inkjets in a wide range of prices, from the HP PhotoSmart 7350 (A4) £150, to the more advanced 7550 with three cartridges, black for text, CMY, and photocolour light cyan, light magenta and black. The 7550 combines excellent photo output with good general-purpose office printer capabilities at a price of £299. The HP PhotoSmart 1215 is an A4 inkjet printer with 2400 × 1200 dpi capability with built-in memory and card reader at £249.

Epson market a variety of units ranging from the inexpensive Stylus C70 at £125, capable of 2880 × 720 dpi, through to the Stylus Photo 925, with optimised resolution of 5760 dpi the highest ever from an inkjet of this class, and variable sized droplet technology with 6 inks, priced at £220. To the Stylus Photo 1290S at £350 with 2880 dpi and 6 colour printing. The Epson Stylus Photo 2100 (A3) with a 2880

× 1440 dpi has 7 individual high capacity pigment based ink cartridges for durability and longevity, priced at £600. The larger format (24 inch wide) printer with 7 colours, CMYK plus light magenta and light cyan and a new light black, is the Epson Stylus Pro 7600. There is a choice between matt black and photo black depending on the type of media being printed. A recent development in inkjets is the printer fitted with a card slot such as the Epson 895DC. This is designed to accept a digital camera memory card directly, without the need to transfer the images to a computer first. An all in one printer, scanner and photocopier with USB interface is the Epson CX3200, this can be purchased at a price of £150! It has 5760 optimised dpi resolution, and up to 600 × 1200 dpi scan resolution. The printing rate is 14 pages per minute in black and about the same in colour, while as a scanner the rate is 10 for black and 9 in colour.

The Canon S900 is a card reader such that one can print directly from the digital camera, it has a resolution of 2440 × 1220 dpi and printing speed of 4 pages per minute (ppm), easy connection via USB, priced at £232.

According to Tinsley[42] the finest quality in inkjet printing is provided by the expensive (£17 000 and upwards) *continuous inkjet* printers. These units force ink under pressure through fine nozzles, one ink for each of four colours, to create a stream of droplets onto paper wrapped on a rotating drum. Continuous ink technology is capable of printing images close to photographic quality, and although capital outlay is expensive they are cheap to run and tolerant of paper quality.

## 7.3 Laser Printers

Laser printers are the best option for correspondence; monochromatic lasers are cheaper to run than inkjets, though more expensive to purchase.

Laser printers use a multi-stage process to turn an electrical signal into an image on paper. The process starts with the printer taking its instructions from the computer in a language that specifies either size and position for text, or graphic information for images. The usual languages are either Postscript or PCL (as used by Hewlett Packard compatibles). If we look at a monochrome laser printer first, it will give some idea of the complexity of design and the reason why they are so much more expensive than, say, inkjets.

As soon as data is received from the computer, the laser printer's internal processor converts this instruction into a bit-map where memory maps every dot of the image. Some laser printers are designated *Windows printers* and do not have their own internal processors, which means the computer has to create the bit-map itself and then write this directly to the printer's memory.

The printing engine is a drum with a coating that allows it to hold an electrostatic charge. The entire surface of the drum is charged by rotating it past an array of high voltage electrodes, and selectively discharged as the drum (which has the same area as the paper onto which the final image will appear) is scanned by a laser diode beam. Every point on the drum is mapped to a point on the sheet of paper passed under it, and selective discharging is done by switching the laser on and off as it scans the drum. Obviously this is a complex process employing optical relays, with printing resolution directly proportional to the size of the laser beam. However, many laser printers are actually LED printers, since they use a row of hundreds of light emitting diodes across the width of the drum, which are then selectively switched on and off (according to image instructions in the printer's memory) as the drum rotates.

The image medium used in laser printing is a *toner* which, for monochrome printing, is a fine black powder. As the drum rotates it picks up the toner at points where its surface remains charged, and since the selective discharge process was mapped according to a *negative* image, a black *positive* image is left on the drum, ready to be transferred to paper. Heat and pressure are now applied to the paper in order to fuse the toner onto the sheet. Finally, after each sheet of paper has been printed, the drum is cleaned off and the process can start again.

It can be seen that such a system will require four drums for CMYK colour, passing the paper from one drum to another! Alternatively, a single drum can be employed with four changes of coloured toner. It is therefore not surprising to find that laser colour printers, in the general sense, are more expensive than Inkjets.

The Canon LBP 1210 is a laser printer at a very modest price. It has a 600 dpi output, which can be taken to 2400 × 600 dpi with automatic image refinement (AIR).

The Hewlett-Packard Colour LaserJet 4600 is a single-pass printer that is as fast in colour (17 ppm) as it is in monochrome. Its resolution is 600 × 600 dpi, enhanced by software (ImageREt) to 2400 dpi. Like most HP colour lasers, the 4600 is designed for a heavy workload, with a monthly duty cycle of 85000 pages. The Hewlett Packard Colour LaserJet 2500 is a professional printer. It prints up to 16 ppm in black and white and 4 ppm in colour.

The Epson EPL-5900 is a compact (A4) mono laser printer with a true 1200 dpi resolution, it can process 12 ppm. Epson have an Aculaser C-2000 which is an A4 colour laser at 600 × 600 dpi, priced at £1878.

The Minolta QMS Magicolor 2300DL, with 2400 × 600 dpi, can give 14 ppm in colour or 16 ppm in monochrome.

The Kyocera Mita FS-1010 is an ideal business entry-level A4 laser It has a 200 MHz processor and will print at 14 ppm. Again, from Kyocera is the Mita FS-1900 which has 18 ppm from its ECOSYS laser and 200 MHz processor.

## 7.4 Dye-sublimation Printers

There can be no doubt that *dye-sublimation* printers produce some of the best digital images and, for professionals at least, at reasonable cost. Indeed, usually a dye-sublimation print cannot be distinguished from a conventional silver halide photograph, particularly in colour.

Dye-sublimation printers require expensive ribbons and special papers, so each print is relatively expensive when compared to that of an inkjet, but then again the quality is far superior. Currently (1997) a decent dye-sublimation printer, such as the Kodak XLS 8600 costs in the region of £6000, which puts it firmly in the professional category. Nevertheless, despite its near photographic quality dye-sublimation prints cannot match the archival permanence of a conventional colour print, and with this in mind Kodak have recently introduced an 'Extra-Life' ribbon which coats the print surface with a transparent protective layer.

Sublimation is a process where a direct transition from solid to vapour can take place without any liquid phase being involved, and the basic principle of a dye-sublimation printer is to use a heated press to drive an image from one material into another. Some dyes and printing inks are able to undergo sublimation, and after being driven into a material as a vapour, can solidify to form an image beneath its surface.

With a dye-sublimation printer the thermal printing head heats a dye ribbon containing a stable base layer and a dye layer. The ribbon actually contains three or four successive dye panels (CMYK), and during operation the dye ribbons are passed sequentially over the thermal head and vapourised as the print-head (heated to 400 °C) passes over each panel. During the contact printing process the dye sublimates, and the gaseous pigment is then absorbed by the polyester resin coating on the printing paper. The temperature of each microscopic pin in the print-head varies the amount of dye used (each dye can be addressed by $2^8$ different temperatures, which results in a possible 16.7 million colours) and colours are fused into the paper with a slight bleeding to allow the dots to merge and so create a dither-free image.

Dye-sublimation papers are specially coated with a gloss or semi-gloss finish, but in order to safeguard the final print, Kodak's 8600 printer automatically applies a final pass through the Ektatherm XtraLife donor, which is a protective laminate on the donor ribbon to guard against moisture, fingerprints, PVC sleeves (which, if damp, can easily strip a colour print of its image layers) and light.

Specifications for the Kodak XLS 8600 quote a 300 pixel per inch resolution and printing speeds (A4) of 78 seconds for CMY colour reflection prints, and 3 minutes for colour transparencies. With the addition of XtraLife these figures are 101 seconds and 2 minutes 36 seconds respectively. Monochrome printing speeds (with XtraLife) are 58 seconds for prints and 71 seconds for transparencies.

Although dye sublimation (correctly known as dye diffusion thermal transfer, or D2T2) may be too expensive for most people, there are always those images that really justify this quality of printing, and in these cases it is a simple matter to send the image file to a printing bureau. Nevertheless, we can expect dye-sublimation printers to come down in price.

## 7.5 Printing: Properties and Papers

The type of printing paper employed is very important to the quality of the finished product. For the Epson Stylus Photo 870, which is the inkjet printer I use, under the heading of properties there is a drop-down menu which indicates dpi. For black and white text the appropriate setting is 360 dpi, for images there is 720 or better still, particularly for colour 1440 dpi. The drop-down menu for the printing paper shows a selection, there is: *Photo quality inkjet paper, Matt paper heavy weight, Premium glossy photo paper, Photo paper* and *Inkjet transparencies.*

In the printing media we have from Epson: Photo Quality Glossy Paper, £8.99p for 20 sheets; Epson Premium Glossy Photo Paper £10.99p for 20 sheets; and Epson Matte Paper-Heavyweight £8.99p for 50 sheets. The matt paper is very good and for every day work is economic and reliable.

Agfa make an inkjet paper which is glossy on one side and satin on the other.

*Fig. 7.2* The Epson PictureMake 6 × 4" dedicated printer.

## 7.6 Dedicated 6 × 4 inch printer

The Epson PictureMate (shown in Fig. 7.2) is a dedicated 6 × 4 colour printer which does not require a computer and printer to produce excellent quality prints. It has provision for all manner of camera cords with loadable storage media ranging from *Compact Flash* to *Smart Media* and is priced at £130. It has numerous facilities including *Zoom* and *Multi-print*.

# 8 Digital Imaging Applications

Just as photography has become an indispensable tool for science, industry, medicine, commerce, research, entertainment, exploration and warfare, so its digital counterpart will provide equal service, but much faster, and with increasing importance and application.

Digital cameras and scanned photographs give the greatest advantage from the computer. Not only can digital images be manipulated much faster than photographs, but they can be analysed much faster too. An important example is the airborne military photograph which, exposed in a hostile environment at some considerable risk, requires the very fastest processing and interpretation. And, although human intelligence will never be replaced, items such as prior knowledge, comparisons, coordinates, image manipulation, background information, metrication and statistics can be interfaced with image data to provide essential answers.

Apart from the wealth of proprietary software available (much of it capable of dealing with just about any subject) there are increasing numbers of customised programs dedicated to supporting imagery with specific applications, such as earth sciences, mapping, astronomy, medicine, physics, etc. The TAL SoftwareWedge™ is a particularly useful package that allows a two-way input/output (I/O) via the RS232 serial port found on all computers. SoftwareWedge can capture data from all manner of laboratory and industrial instruments, and can add serial data acquisition and instrument control to any Windows application without additional programming. With this type of software any image can be supported with graphs, charts and tables, with information taken directly from the image itself.

There can be no doubt that tomorrow's users of photography will use digital cameras exclusively; just as publishers now expect their authors to supply manuscripts on disk, so will they expect photographs on the same medium. Nevertheless, we can expect conventional methods to remain for a long time yet, mainly because film currently offers one or two advantages over digital systems, but in general the future belongs to the digital camera.

The amateur photographer will seek his/her choice of medium according to interest. But it is already obvious that many are taking a fresh interest in their hobby, as digital cameras and software become less expensive.

The professional (commercial) photographer has already seen the writing on the wall, and few would argue they could continue business outside of the new technology. But for the most part it is the professional (non-photographer) who sees the digital camera for its true worth. As the industrial and scientific photographer has steadily found less work over the past twenty years (mainly because of increased technology) only the medical photographer seems to have survived as a technical specialist within the profession. Today everyone is a photographer, yet very few have seen the inside of a darkroom, let alone exposed a black and white photograph! Nevertheless, within a few days they can master digital technology and experiment with their own creativity (in colour or monochrome) to produce prints with a quality limited only by cost. For this reason, the following list of digital imaging applications includes many professions other than that of the professional photographer.

## 8.1 Press Photography and Photo-journalism

Press work is perhaps the most readily understood area of photography, mainly because it intercepts everyone's life at some stage or other, and also because it's a major source of news gathering. Press photography is extremely competitive of course and, although the work can be interesting, it is also very demanding. The practitioner has to be prepared for any environment—interiors, exteriors, harsh or benign —the accent is always on speed of image capture and speed of transmission to the editorial desk.

With photo-journalism there is perhaps less demand for speed, and more demand for image quality. But in both fields everything and anything is to be expected. For this reason it is important to select the right tool for the job.

Traditionally the camera (or rather the equipment) has to include a number of lenses, a flash gun, filters, rolls of film, and (sensibly) a portable tripod. All of these can easily be realised with most high-quality digital units because they are based on conventional 35 mm cameras, and they can certainly offer comparable quality. But this misses the point entirely!

The prime advantage of handling digital images is speed! Subsequent to exposure, images can be immediately downloaded to a laptop computer where they can be cropped, enhanced, modified and re-sized, then transmitted via a modem and digital mobile telephone to the newsdesk. Such methods are already being used of course, and even packaged as a complete system for this purpose,[43] mainly with cameras like the Canon EOS 1DS, the Nikon D1X, Fuji FinePix S2 Pro, Kodak DCS-760 and Canon EOS D60, all of which offer professional 35 mm camera quality and good shutter speeds, most of which provide for fast burst rates and high ISO speeds. High ISO speeds are very important for press work and, although all of these cameras allow for an ISO equivalent of at least 400 (colour) and some of them up to 1600. As with film, the digital equivalent ISO speed is important for press work, since fast subject movement can only be arrested with high shutter speeds, and if the problem is compounded with low light levels, the press camera needs all the 'film speed' it can muster.

A typical commercial or high street photographer will need to select a digital camera that can satisfy the many and varied tasks it has to do. In this respect I contacted a good friend who owns a photographic business which deals with every possible application of photography. John Bigglestone and Company (see App: C) of Devizes, Wilts, selected the Fuji Finepix S2 Pro for taking those unexpected shots when out on location. Satisfactory dynamic range is desirable in all digital cameras, but in the S2 it is particularly good, as shown in Fig. 8.1 (colour section) where highlights, colour and deep shadows prevail in this photo-journalism record of a forge, with electronic flash.

## 8.2 Commercial and Industrial Photography

Although perhaps wanting for a better definition, commercial photography has long been understood to include work such as that carried out by high-street photographic studios, fashion and advertising agencies and, in some establishments, industrial photography.

Just as high-street photographers have been offering wedding videos for many years, so they now offer CD-ROM images taken from either conventional film or digital cameras. One particular company of interest is the London-based Multimedia Factory which offers the 'Forever Yours' service consisting of a 50-image wedding CD, complete with customised captions and music. Any established wedding photographer wishing to offer this service to his/her clients can do so by acting as an agent for 'Forever Yours' on a commission basis.

A number of studios specialising in high-quality catalogue and brochure photography are now seeing the advantage of digital cameras, and have invested in expensive systems such as the Phase One Studio Kit, and the Leaf Lumina, with images processed in Photoshop. For the main part it has meant a considerable capital outlay, new lighting and fresh expertise, but financial advantage comes from increased efficiency, time saving and improved products. All the same a decent digital camera such as the Fuji S2, not costing too much, can produce quality studio portraiture like that shown in Fig. 8.2 (colour section) which was taken by John Bigglestone using the S2 with Nikon 80–200 mm and studio electronic flash.

An increasing number of manufacturers and industrialists are using digital cameras for various tasks ranging from simple data recording to sophisticated research systems. Examples in the former category include the use of a Kodak DCS-420 for providing a spare-parts database in the transport industry[44] and for log tracking in forestry.[45]

In advertising photography, a highly specialised industry where quality must be observed, we can again look to digital. The S2 shot (John Bigglestone and Company) of Fig. 8.3 (colour section), was taken with the 80–200 mm Nikon lens and studio electronic flash, and manipulated and enhanced in Photoshop. The facilities offered by Photoshop are truly remarkable, whereas days of hard work in the darkroom can be conducted in minutes by an experienced worker on the computer.

The industrial shot in Fig. 8.4 (colour section), is a panorama consisting of six images taken with the Fuji S2, to show an old engineering shop before the firm moved to new premises. The panorama was manipulated in Photoshop by John Bigglestone and Partners. Photo taken with an S2 fitted with a Nikon 35–70 mm lens.

## 8.3 Holographic Interferometry

Although holography normally requires extremely high-resolution photographic plates to form a three-dimensional image, holographic interference fringes can be recorded with far less resolution, even with the inferior quality of a frame-grabbed video image of 512 × 480 pixels, provided that a reference hologram of the subject is already available. A particular system of interest is that employed for the vibration testing of propeller blades used on cruise missiles, and for detecting cracks in space shuttle heat shield tiles,[46] where a typical holographic interferometric arrangement (see Fig. 8.5) is recorded by a digital system rather than a holographic plate. Commercial users of these systems include Boeing and McDonnell-Douglas among many others who use interferometry for routine non-destructive testing.

Although true holograms (three-dimensional images, exhibiting parallax) are constructed on the principle of optical interference, with primary fringe spacing recorded at the micro-resolution level (<1 μm), a holographic interferometer only looks at the secondary fringes, which have spacings large enough to enable fringes to be counted by the human eye, as shown in Fig. 8.6. These secondary fringes can then be recorded by a relatively low-resolution CCD imager.

A basic interferometric layout is shown in Fig. 8.5, where a 30 mW HeNe laser has split-beams $I_r$ (reference beam) and $I_o$ (object beam) meeting at the holographic plate $P$. An object under test is placed at $O$ and angles $\alpha$ and $\beta$ measured from the motion vector $OZ$.[47][48]

With the object ($O$) in position the reflected object beam ($I_o$) interferes with the reference beam ($I_r$) to create primary fringes, and when subsequently developed the hologram reveals a 3-D image of the object when placed in its original position at $P$ and illuminated with the same reference beam. With the object beam blanked-off, the hologram's virtual image is revealed and by careful adjustment this can then be accurately superimposed upon the object. If the object is now changed in shape by any means, and re-illuminated by $I_o$, then hologram and object differences are revealed as a system of secondary fringes, as shown in Fig. 8.6.

In Fig. 8.6, we have an overloaded 2 μF (275 V) paper capacitor with fringes recorded by 'time-lapsed' (or double-exposure) interferometric holography using the set-up shown in Fig. 8.5 (not to scale). First, a record was made with the subject

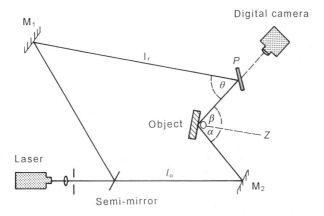

*Fig. 8.5* Holographic arrangement suitable for optical interference recording. Although not elaborated in the diagram, the laser beam is expanded by the lens and spatial filter placed immediately in front of the beam-splitting semi-mirror.

*Fig 8.6.* Coarse interference fringes are easily recorded by a low-resolution CCD imager. This sujbect: a 2 µF (275 V) paper capacitor under voltage overload.

unloaded, then another exposure was made with the capacitor overloaded to 500 volts.[47] The resulting double exposure then gave secondary interference fringes due to changes in the skin of the capacitor.

Referring to Fig. 8.5 and Fig. 8.6, the measured change in state is taken along the motion vector (*OZ*) and has amplitude $\Delta Z$ given by:

$$\Delta Z = n\lambda/(\cos\,\alpha + \cos\,\beta) \tag{8.1}$$

where:

$n$ is the fringe order number,
$\lambda$ is the wavelength of the laser (HeNe = 632.8 nm).

To find the value of $n$, the count must proceed from the zero-order fringe ($n = 0$) which can usually be found by scanning across the reconstructed image (thus varying $\beta$) causing the fringes to move except where $n = 0$. For Fig. 8.6, the zero order was found to be at the edge of the capacitor and counting into closed fringe contours, $n$ was observed to be 13. With $\alpha = 20°$ and $\beta = 26°$, Eq: 8.1 then gave a displacement value of 4.45 µm.

With the digital variant of this system, the only difference is that the subject's second exposure is recorded by a low-resolution CCD imager, and analysed through a computer. Whereas the method just described is known as *time-lapsed interferometry*, similar systems (using the same optical set-up) are known as *real-time interferometry* (where fringes are observed and can be recorded in real-time), and *time-averaged interferometry* (where vibratory deformation can be exposed while the object is actually vibrating). For the non-destructive testing of vibrating propeller blades, the method used is time-averaged interferometry.

### Minolta Dimage V camera

A novel digital camera produced by Minolta incorporates a rotating detachable ×2.7 zoom lens that will certainly be useful for recording otherwise inaccessible areas in industrial photography.

The Minolta Dimage V has a built-in 1.8 inch colour LCD (liquid crystal display) monitor, and a removable SmartMedia memory card of 2 Mb capacity. The CCD sensor is a full-frame 640 × 480 pixel chip and up to 16 images can be stored in fine JPEG compression mode. Computer interface is via RS232C, and an integral flash unit (Guide Number of 10) supports a 100 ISO sensitivity. However, the most important aspect of this camera is the detachable zoom lens which, extended on a one metre cable, is capable of looking around corners and into areas normally impossible to photograph.

## 8.4 Medical Photography

There are few scientific disciplines that employ photography and digital imaging more than medicine, where it is used for patients' records, teaching, surgery, pathology, research and diagnosis. For over 100 years, photography has served medicine well, and has allowed clinicians to evaluate medical images exposed under an EMR (electromagnetic radiation) extending from X-rays to the near-infrared, with instruments ranging from the humble camera to the electron microscope.

Owing to the size of subjects ecountered in medical imaging, much of the work is table-top technology that comes under the general heading of macro-imaging. And, for smaller than macro-sized specimens, special tools such as the optical microscope and endoscope are required. All teaching hospitals and medical research centres rely on medical imaging, and usually have specially qualified staff dedicated to this work.

Digital imaging is not only an extension of well-established photographic techniques, but also a very useful method for putting images into patients' files along with related data. Wherever a photographic camera can be put to a task, so can the digital camera—even to fluorescent microscopy!

One of the first departments to use digital imaging (1993) was the Medical Illustration Unit at the Institute of Child Health, Great Ormond Street, London, where they pioneered the inclusion of digital images in patients' medical records.

Since the Patients' Charter came into effect (allowing all patients access to their medical records) it has become more and more important to keep these records up to date, and digital imaging is ideal for this purpose. At Great Ormond Street for example, a large proportion of the patients are recorded digitally, using the Kodak EOS.DCS-3 camera and Kodak 8600 printer. One of the main attributes of the digital camera system is speed, particularly since the Patients' Charter states that information has to be turned around as quickly as possible. At the City Hospital, Truro, Cornwall, where they employ the Kodak DCS-420, they find that turn-around with a digital system is between 6 and 12 hours, whereas with film it can be up to three days!

Digital imaging extends throughout the entire medical scene, including opthalmology, dentistry, anatomy, physiology and X-ray; it is now common to use digital cameras to record X-ray screened images.

Digital cameras are also invaluable in the ambulance service, where paramedics use digital cameras to record accident scenes. These images are then transmitted to hospital via digital mobile telephone, so that doctors can see the extent of injuries incurred and allow treatments to be planned in advance.[49]

## Face scanning

An interesting medical innovation that has also proved itself in fields other than medicine is a scanner system for digitising human body surfaces. Developed by Dr Alfred Linney (Head of Medical Graphics) and his team at the Department of Medical Physics and Bioengineering, University College London, the system records facial surfaces and is based on the principle of triangulation.[50]

Motivated from an idea that computer graphics might be used to simulate and predict facial surgery, the optical face scanner is widely used in reconstructive surgery to correct badly deformed faces, and for a variety of forensic and anthropometric studies.

The basic principle of the scanning system is shown in Fig. 8.7, where a line of laser light is seen to be projected on to the facial surface. Viewed obliquely, the line

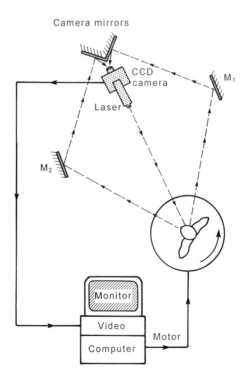

*Fig. 8.7* Face Scanner system with CCD imager, developed at University College London.

appears distorted, reflecting the shape of the surface anatomy. This distorted line is then recorded by a CCD camera connected to a computer via a customised interface board. The mirror arrangement shown in Fig. 8.7 allows the line to be viewed by the camera from two opposing directions, which is necessary to avoid loss of data caused by the occlusion of parts of the facial surface by the prominence of the nose. Using a video camera and frame-grabber (Panasonic 6200), camera signals are pre-processed by the interface board. For each TV frame a set of digital numbers is generated, representing the mid-point of the pulses on the video scan lines produced by the projected laser line. A calibration programme converts these numbers into spatial coordinates of points lying along the laser line illuminating the surface.

To scan the surface of a face (or body), the subject is rotated on a platform under computer control and, for a face, the platform is usually rotated through 200° in a 15 second period, but both speed and extent of rotation may be varied according to subject. Up to 256 profiles may be recorded per scan, and the angles at which these are recorded may be programmed according to the detail required. Something between 30 000 and 60 000 three-dimensional coordinates of points lying on the anatomical surface are usually collected in a single scan, the points being recorded with a precision better than 0.5 mm.

For low-cost medical reports, images are produced in TIFF and faces can be reproduced with any desired view as shown in Fig. 8.8. Used in conjunction with X-ray computed tomography and other medical imaging systems, the optical scanning system shown in Fig. 8.7 assists in a number of applications including; surgery, diagnostic radiology, prosthesis and implant design, clinical growth studies, forensic science, archaeology, psychology and training. In addition, the system also generates the data necessary to drive a numerically controlled milling machine to cut out a three-dimensional model of any image displayed on the monitor.

*Fig. 8.8* Two views selected from the digitally imaged scan of a subject's face. From the scan file of any face, it is a simple matter to reconstruct selected viewpoints from the system's software, and print hard copies, as shown here. Images courtesy of Dr A. Linney, Medical Physics and Bio-Engineering Department, University College London.

## 8.5 Forensic Science and Police Work

The camera has always been a useful tool in forensic science and, from examples taken from other disciplines, it seems natural to assume that digital cameras may offer considerable advantages to Scenes of Crime Officers and forensic scientists, where images and audio records could be made quickly, and where a satisfactory result could be confirmed before evidence is lost through difficulties such as bad weather, or other uncontrolled situations. Nevertheless, the digital camera has yet to be employed by UK Scenes of Crime Officers and, although one can expect the situation to change at some time in the future, there are significant problems associated with digital recording in this particular field.

Unlike most imaging applications, forensic records are always open to argument in a court of law where, if an image is to be accepted, it must be above legal criticism. For most purposes we have seen that digital images can equal photographic quality, either monochrome or colour. Indeed, we have seen (Fig. 2.9) that digital cameras exhibit tonal linearity unequalled by silver halide imagery, so in this respect they have a great advantage. But in certain areas digital systems are flawed by their very character.

Although conventional silver halide materials can be considered isotropic (exhibiting physical properties independent of direction), a CCD array (with an $x$, $y$ matrix of pixels) is a non-isotropic medium that can introduce aliasing problems in some images. As a consequence there is a natural reluctance to employ a system that could be questioned in a court of law. Indeed, this problem has already been investigated with respect to fingerprint records where, according to Roy Thompson of the Home Office, Police Scientific Development Branch,[51] there is evidence that digitised records of fingerprints exhibit prohibitive aliasing errors, and for this application digital cameras and scanning techniques are not recommended. For a full sized fingerprint (about 2 cm wide) a scanning resolution of 500 dpi is recommended, but most prints lifted from a scene of crime are only a fraction of this size, and so a resolution of at least 1000 dpi is considered necessary! These are very stringent conditions of course, and ones that will require a degree of 'overscanning' to avoid Nyquist limitations (Eq: 3.10). Even so, it's possible that high-resolution cameras such as Kodak's DCS-460 may prove useful in this respect.

The laser scanning system shown in Fig. 8.7 is also used in forensic work where, not infrequently, a skull is found in suspicious circumstances and needs to be identified. To perform a reconstruction of the face the skull is scanned, and a scan is taken of a face of an individual of similar type to that inferred from the skull. The facial surface is then adapted to the skull using accepted tables of mean soft tissue thicknesses. Aquaintances of missing persons are then asked to view the reconstructed facial image.

The 3-D dataset produced by the optical scanner has also been used to confirm identification of suspects recorded on security cameras, where the shape and proportions of the face of the accused can be compared with those found in the security images. A single optical scan may then be used to provide good silhouettes of the face as depicted from all of the viewpoints shown in the video recording.

Turning to less esoteric applications, up to a dozen police forces within the UK are already using digital cameras for tracking millions of drivers along British roads. With the help of sophisticated software, these cameras can read a passing number-plate and automatically check it against a police database of known or suspected offenders. A digital camera placed above and behind the traffic flow, can read several plates at once using the Racal Talon system, which has successfully been tested on major motorways since 1993.

Other agencies employing digital surveillance cameras include HM Customs & Excise, who similarly log every vehicle entering the UK.

## 8.6  Military Applications

All military photographers are trained at the Joint School of Photography at RAF Cosford and, whereas this course was initially for Royal Air Force personnel only, it has been the main source of photographic instruction for all three armed forces for a number of years now. All photographers are trained in conventional photographic techniques, and digital cameras form an important part of the training.

Army personnel will, on completion of their course, be transferred to the Royal Logistics Corps of Photographers, and some could end up at the Public Relations Office at HQ Land Command, where their work is based around digital imaging systems. As photo-journalists, the modern Army's two-man public relations teams carry all their kit in a suitcase containing a Nikon E2 or DS-515 digital camera, PCMCIA cards, modems, Apple Mac computer, Powerbook 5300ce scanner, and small satellite telephones plus a portable generator. The advantage of digital is of course speed, particularly when military news events need to be transmitted as quickly as possible, but the majority of work is still done with colour film, which is processed in a portable darkroom before being scanned.[52]

The RAF (and other Air Forces) also employ digital cameras for general work, but their main interest is in the more serious role of airborne reconnaissance. Naturally little is known about these applications, but some idea of their importance can be gained from known use of these cameras in aerial mapping and remote sensing.

Current investigations by US military forces include trials with a modified Kodak DCS-100 camera for reconnaissance in low threat areas such as Bosnia and Somalia.[53] Known as the tactical airborne digital camera system (TADCS) this camera, complete with 105 mm lens, has been operated by the Radar Intercept Officer of US navy F-14 aircrews for tasks suited to pre-strike reconnaissance, and from P-3 aircraft for monitoring shipping and counter narcotics operations. According to this report, image quality does not equal that provided by conventional photo-recce cameras carried in the usual F-14 pods, but TADCS imagery can be relayed back to ship, or land base, in under 30 seconds by a line-of-sight UHF data link effective up to 300 km. The TADCS allows up to 24 images to be taken in a single burst, all of them being stored in the system's hard disk. Up to 150 images can be stored on the hard disk and, once clear of the operational area, aircrew are able to review and select images on a tactical information display screen. From here it is a simple matter to compress image data and relay it back to base via an encryption unit.

## 8.7  Aerial Surveys and Remote Sensing

Conventional topographic mapping is done with large format cameras such as the Zeiss RMK top around, and when we say *large* we are talking about a 23 × 23 cm format air camera that costs around 400 000 for a top-of-the-range unit complete with navigation interface, navigation sight and various other bits of advanced technology.

Useful air mapping can also be done with good-quality 35 mm cameras, but obviously there are limitations, or why do we use such large and expensive air cameras?

Small format aerial photography (SFAP) has come of age at a time when large format air cameras have never been more sophisticated or expensive. As a consequence, survey missions using large format must reflect these costs which, for many clients, are totally prohibitive. Naturally SFAP can only satisfy those requirements that do not demand photogrammetric cover extending over large areas, but this still leaves a number of tasks that require neither metric accuracy nor extensive survey, and it is in these areas that SFAP is both useful and economic.[54]

The main reason for using 23 cm format is because it covers a larger area (footprint) on the ground, whereas a 35 mm camera (for the same photo-scale) covers only 1.6% of the same area. Needless to say a digital camera is even more restrictive, and for equal scale the DCS-460 (27.6 × 18.4 mm format) covers only about 1% of the large format footprint. Nevertheless, by using wide angle lenses (24 mm or less) the digital camera has proved to be an effective means for remote sensing, and for mapping small areas.

## Digital mapping with the Kodak DCS-460 camera

In cooperation with the Department of GeoTechnologies, at University College Bath Spa, Bath, I have an on-going programme investigating the use of various digital cameras and aircraft for topographic mapping. The DCS-460 CIR camera was the first camera after the DCS-420 CIR to be examined. The DCS-420 CIR was capable of only 0.24% of the large format footprint (9.2 mm × 14 mm), apart from its unequal dimensions which, with the DCSD-460, made it difficult to calculate the necessary planning. The DCS-460 CIR is shown in Fig. 5.10.

The important calculations for a line-overlap survey are those which determine scale number ($m_b$), ground coverage ($S$), base ($b$), for a given forward overlap ($p$), and the time interval between exposures ($\Delta T$) for a given ground speed of the aircraft.

$$m_b = H_g/f \qquad (8.2)$$

where:

$H_g$ is the height above ground,
$f$ is the focal length of camera lens.

$$S = m_b S' \qquad (8.3)$$

where:

$S$ is the length of side of ground covered,
$S'$ is the side of image format.

$$b = S(1 - p/100) \qquad (8.4)$$

where:

$b$ is the base (ground distance between centre of one image and the next),
$p$ is the percentage of forward overlap.

$$\Delta T = b/V_g \qquad (8.5)$$

where:

$\Delta T$ is in seconds,

$V_g$ is the ground speed of the aircraft in metres/second.

The principal benchmark for any new air mapping or reconnaissance system is resolution. One of the main questions to be answered from trials concerning digital cameras for aerial work was what may be expected from an off-the-shelf camera. According to Eq: 5.3 we can expect an image resolution of 22 LP/mm (for 9 μm pixels) which, when translated to the ground via the scale number of, say, 20000, gives a ground resolution of 90 cm (1/22 mm × 20 000).

But it is well known in aerial survey and military reconnaissance that we can detect and recognise ground detail much smaller than that predicted by expressions such as Eq: 5.3. For one thing, small differences in colour are seen much better than those in monochrome, and lineaments are seen much better than complex subjects. As a consequence, it is now common to quantify spatial resolution in satellite and remote sensing imagery in terms of the ground sampled distance (GSD) which, although lacking scientific rigour, provides a convenient figure of merit and one that seems likely to be adopted for digital aerial imaging.[55] Rather than quantifying resolved *image* detail, GSD is a measure of the resolved *ground* detail, and is calculated from the product of image spread function (ISF) and scale number, as:

$$GSD = (ISF)m_b \tag{8.6}$$

Applying Eq: 8.6 to the DCS-460 imagery under discussion we can, with some reservations,[56] replace the ISF with pixel size, to give a fair approximation as:

$$GSD \approx (Px)m_b \tag{8.7}$$

For a nominal scale number of 20 000 this results in a GSD of 9 μm × 20 000 ≈ 18 cm. It was possible to check this value from the colour images of broken barn roof, where a 15 cm beam, is clearly resolved from the print of 17 000 scale.

## *Airborne remote sensing with digital cameras*

With a spectral sensitivity equal to that of silver halide materials (see Fig. 5.4), CCD cameras are particularly well suited to the role of remote sensing since much of this work is done over relatively small areas, and images can be accessed very swiftly.

Whereas large area remote sensing is adequately covered by satellite imagery (and has been since 1972 with the launch of LANDSAT 1), with continuing cover from LANDSAT's 4 and 5, plus the 10 metre resolution SPOT imagery, it is often necessary to supplement satellite data with airborne remote sensing in order to gain better detail for a particular surveillance.

The basic principle behind remote sensing imagery is to sample specific terrain features and crops with various bands of EMR. Using various types of film (colour, infrared, panchromatic and false-colour infrared) in conjunction with narrow-band filters and an array of cameras, multispectral photography (MSP) provides a valuable remote sensing technique, particularly when applied in a multi-temporal mode.[57][58] For most purposes a panchromatic film with a Kodak narrow-cut red number 29 red filter, and monochrome infrared film with a number 87 infrared filter will suffice. Analysis is mainly a question of comparision between the red and infrared records:

where infrared is strongly absorbed by moisture, and highly reflected by healthy organic matter (chlorophyll), the red record can then be used as a control. I found this simple two-channel technique to be both economic and satisfactory in studies such as disease in wheat crops.[57]

## Multispectral photography with DCS-420 CIR and DCS-460 CIR cameras

The Remote Sensing and Geographic Information Systems (RSGIS) Unit, Bath College of Higher Education, is a small but very experienced group who use digital MSP techniques both abroad and within the UK. Headed by Alexander Koh the RSGIS Unit employs a DCS-460 CIR (colour infrared) model for research and development in this area, also a DCS-420 CIR. Most of the imagery is processed in Photoshop from images stored in PCMCIA (Type III) cards, where MSP images are merged to produce false-colour products and mosaics. The measurement of ground features being done with the aid of VirtuoZo, a computer based photogrammetric machine.

The RSGIS camera assembly was put together by Alex Koh, and incorporates a drift mount with timer for sequenced line-overlap surveys. The DCS-460 CIR records spectral data in the green, red and near infrared simply by changing from the normal (interpolated) colour filters found in the conventional model to a composite which includes an infrared filter, it being remembered that the spectral response of the M5 (DCS-420) and M6 (DCS-460) chip extends to 1000 nm! The camera also comes with a tri-port adaptor for plugging in the shutter cable release and also a GPS receiver.

The DCS-460 CIR camera is an interesting device, and will certainly be of interest to many who require a reliable MSP system that can be processed quickly, even in flight! The development of this camera is said to have started at the suggestion of the US Forest Service, who requested Kodak to produce a digital equivalent to the well-known false-colour infrared film they market. Since then it has been used for numerous forestry and riparian projects, as well as for applications more related to law enforcement than earth sciences. This point is made clear by Fig. 8.9 (see colour section), where a helicopter-borne DCS-420 CIR has been used to record an illegal plot of cannabis hidden within a forest. The bright red cluster of plants near the centre of Fig. 8.9 is easily detected.

## Kodak DCS-460 C/CIR camera

Currently the best digital camera available for mapping and remote sensing is the DCS-460 C/CIR model, I say currently but the camera has not been in production since 2001. Yet it remains the best camera for the job and is still the best CIR camera available. The C stands for colour and CIR for the integrated colour infrared option. This camera is specially designed for Kodak's Aerial Systems division and can be purchased only against a special order.

It has a 27.6 × 18.4 mm sized chip and this larger format covers a greater footprint than the 420 series, given the same 28 mm lens and flying height. Although image capture is rather slow (one frame per 12 seconds) this period can be reduced if the best quality PCMCIA card is used. The DCS-460 C/CIR has only one exposure-speed rating and that is 80 ISO.

There is no doubt that the DCS-460 C/CIR can provide image quality equal to that of many colour films and although the M6 chip (Kodak Sensor KAF 6301) has the same 9 μm square pixels as the M5 used in the 420 series, the improved CFA interpolation used in the 460 C/CIR facilitates much higher image resolution.

## Mapping and remote sensing with the DCS-460 C/CIR camera

In early 2000 Alex Koh and I made a remote sensing aerial survey of the Freeport Copper mine in Iryan Jaya, western New Guinea. The operation was difficult due to the height of the mine (12000 feet) which usually was covered in broken cloud and mist. Although only 4 degrees below the equator it was nearly one week before we had a reasonably clear sky for photography. We were tasked with photographs of the mine plus six glaciers close by. These are the Cartensz Glaciers, and they were getting smaller as the years passed by. The camera was the DCS-460 CIR which was mounted on the port step of a Bell 412 helicopter, and operated from the cabin. The two PCMCIA cards allowed us 80 shots per card and we operated the survey (with 60% stereoscopic cover) at 18000 feet. This was followed by numerous surveys over the jungle floor covering new towns, malarial sites, levees and native relocation areas, at various scales. Our operation started at 0600 hours from our basecamp airstrip at Timika, in the coastal swamp area, by 1000 hrs flying was unproductive due to the weather. The copper mine is shown in Fig. 8.10 (see colour section).

## DCS-460 C/CIR camera calibration

All air cameras used for photogrammetry must be calibrated. This was done by Alex Koh using a special target projected onto a laboratory wall, 16 images from various camera stations were taken and then uploaded into the EOS Systems Photomodeler software for automatic camera calibration. A typical camera calibration is shown in Fig. 8.11, for the DCS-460 CIR camera and 28 mm lens. It can be seen that the calibrated focal length is shown as 28.4566, and the radial distortions are plotted.

## Kodak DCS-Pro Back (MF-DMC II )

It will be recalled (Chapter 5) that the DCS-Pro-Back was ideal for aerial survey since it has a square format. When used in this application it is calibrated, equipped with a sequence timer, and with a drift mount that is vibration free and is known as the MF-DMC II. A typical aerial survey starting from a position in Lyme Regis and going east to Charmouth, Dorset, was planned at a scale of 1 : 30 000 with a 40 mm Zeiss Distagon lens. A 60% forward overlap of images (27 in all) secured the stereoscopic cover and the flying height above ground was 4000 feet, with four runs as shown by Fig. 8.12 (see colour section). The camera, a Hasselblad 555ELD with Kodak Pro Back of 4072 × 4072 Px (16 MPx) and 40 mm lens is shown in Fig. 8.13. The calibration report is shown in Fig. 8.14 and a typical photograph in the Charmouth area is shown by Fig. 8.15 (see colour section).

# 8.8 Applications in Astronomy

Perhaps astronomy should have been mentioned first in this list of applications, since it was here that CCD imagers were first put to serious use in the mid-1970s. There are

**Camera calibration parameters**

**Lens characteristics**

| | |
|---|---|
| s/n lens | 415876 |
| f-stop | 4 |
| s/n camera | 460-R015 |
| fl | 28.4566 mm |
| dim AT | 27.5473 mm |
| dim XT | 18.3240 mm |
| PPx ref TLHC | 14.131700 mm |
| PPy ref TLHC | 8.938100 mm |
| PPx ref Centre Line | 0.358050 mm |
| PPy ref Centre Line | 0.223900 mm |
| K1 | 1.669E-04 |
| K2 | -3.853E-07 |

| radius [mm] | azimuth [rads] | x [mm] | y [mm] | dr [mm] |
|---|---|---|---|---|
| 0.000000 | 0.000000 | 0.000000 | 0.000000 | 0.000000 |
| 1.000000 | 0.174533 | 0.173648 | 0.984808 | 0.000167 |
| 2.000000 | 0.349066 | 0.684040 | 1.879385 | 0.000661 |
| 3.000000 | 0.523599 | 1.500000 | 2.598076 | 0.001471 |
| 4.000000 | 0.698132 | 2.571150 | 3.064178 | 0.002572 |
| 5.000000 | 0.872665 | 3.830222 | 3.213938 | 0.003932 |
| 6.000000 | 1.047198 | 5.196152 | 3.000000 | 0.005509 |
| 7.000000 | 1.221730 | 6.577848 | 2.394141 | 0.007253 |
| 8.000000 | 1.396263 | 7.878462 | 1.389185 | 0.009103 |
| 9.000000 | 1.570796 | 9.000000 | 0.000000 | 0.010991 |
| 10.000000 | 1.745329 | 9.848078 | -1.736482 | 0.012837 |
| 11.000000 | 1.919862 | 10.336619 | -3.762222 | 0.014554 |
| 12.000000 | 2.094395 | 10.392305 | -6.000000 | 0.016044 |
| 13.000000 | 2.268928 | 9.958578 | -8.356239 | 0.017202 |

**DCS 460CIR-R015**

*Fig. 8.11* Camera Calibration for Photogrammetry of the 28.4566 mm lens and the DCS-460 CIR. Calibration report by: Alexander Koh.

few keen amateur astronomers today who have not put a CCD camera at the end of their telescope (particularly since these can now be purchased for something like £300), and the use of CCD cameras in professional astronomy is universal. Many of these CCD cameras have exceptional sensitivity, and can record the image of a nebula or galaxy as much as 30 times faster than photographic film.

CCDs are now the most widely used optical sensor at all major astronomical observatories and, as low-light-level detectors, they are both sensitive and stable with signal sensitivities almost at the single electron level. The CCD is now an essential component of modern astronomical instrumentation, as may be appreciated when one recalls that the Hubble Space Telescope uses CCDs to achieve high-resolution images from space. Indeed, one of the most remarkable properties of the CCD camera is its ability to penetrate into deep space and turn the telescope into a virtual time machine, as witnessed by CCD images such as those of *Abell 2065 in Corona Borealis*, where a cluster of galaxies are so remote their light takes over a billion ($10^9$) years to reach the camera.[59]

*Fig. 8.13* The MF-DMC II. A Kodak Pro Back fitted to a Hasselblad 555 ELD, with the camera and lens (40 mm Zeiss Distagon) calibrated for the photogrammetric purpose. This 16 MPx camera is ideal for aerial survey and has 4072 × 4072 pixels.

**Geotechnologies Camera Calibration for Medium Format Digital Mapping Camera**
*User changeable items are coded red and highlighted yellow.*
*Geotechnologies accept no responsibility for the use of this utility.*

Camera calibration certificate

| | | | | |
|---|---|---|---|---|
| s/n lens | 8888791 | Lens type | Carl Zeiss Distagon 4/40 T* | |
| s/n camera | DCSPB-00310 | CCD pixel size [mm] | 0.009000 | along flight track (x-axis) |
| f-stop | 5.6 | CCD array size AT [pixels] | 4072 | |
| dimension AT [mm] | 36.6480 | CCD array size [pixels] | 4072 | |
| dimension XT [mm] | 36.6480 | | | across |
| PPx ref TLHC [mm] | 18.9110 | *NOTES:* | | flight |
| PPy ref TLHC [mm] | 18.4841 | 1. Distortion is positive if away from coordinate centre line | | track |
| K1 | 3.642E-05 | 2. Calibrated at a temperature of 20 Celcius | | (y-axis) |
| K2 | -2.262E-08 | 3. No filter fitted | | |

| angle [deg] | angle [rads] | radius [mm] | dr [mm] | Measurements | | |
|---|---|---|---|---|---|---|
| 0.000 | 0.000000 | 0.0 | 0.000000 | Calibrated Principal Distance [mm] | 41.1785 | |
| 13.846 | 0.241661 | 1.0 | 0.000036 | Coordinates Centre Line [mm] | 0.0000 | 0.0000 |
| 27.692 | 0.483322 | 2.0 | 0.000145 | Principal Point ref Centre Line (x,y) [mm] | 0.5870 | -0.1601 |
| 41.538 | 0.724983 | 3.0 | 0.000326 | | | |
| 55.385 | 0.966644 | 4.0 | 0.000577 | Fiducial BLHC pixel centre (x,y) [mm] | -18.3195 | -18.3195 |
| 69.231 | 1.208305 | 5.0 | 0.000896 | Fiducial TLHC pixel centre (x,y) [mm] | -18.3195 | 18.3195 |
| 83.077 | 1.449966 | 6.0 | 0.001282 | Fiducial TRHC pixel centre (x,y) [mm] | 18.3195 | 18.3195 |
| 96.923 | 1.691627 | 7.0 | 0.001730 | Fiducial BRHC pixel centre (x,y) [mm] | 18.3195 | -18.3195 |
| 110.769 | 1.933288 | 8.0 | 0.002238 | | | |
| 124.615 | 2.174949 | 9.0 | 0.002802 | Date of calibration [dd/mm/yyyy] | 06/03/2002 | |
| 138.462 | 2.416610 | 10.0 | 0.003416 | s/n lens & camera | 8888791 | DCSPB-00310 |
| 152.308 | 2.658271 | 11.0 | 0.004076 | | | |
| 166.154 | 2.899932 | 12.0 | 0.004775 | **Radial Distortion** | | |
| 180.000 | 3.141593 | 13.0 | 0.005509 | | | |
| 193.846 | 3.383254 | 14.0 | 0.006269 | | | |
| 207.692 | 3.624915 | 15.0 | 0.007049 | | | |
| 221.538 | 3.866576 | 16.0 | 0.007841 | | | |
| 235.385 | 4.108237 | 17.0 | 0.008636 | | | |
| 249.231 | 4.349898 | 18.0 | 0.009426 | | | |
| 263.077 | 4.591558 | 19.0 | 0.010200 | | | |
| 276.923 | 4.833219 | 20.0 | 0.010949 | | | |
| 290.769 | 5.074880 | 21.0 | 0.011662 | | | |
| 304.615 | 5.316541 | 22.0 | 0.012328 | | | |
| 318.462 | 5.558202 | 23.0 | 0.012936 | Radius [mm] | | |
| 332.308 | 5.799863 | 24.0 | 0.013473 | | | |
| 346.154 | 6.041524 | 25.0 | 0.013927 | | | |

*Fig. 8.14* Calibration report for the medium format MF-DMC II with 40 mm lens. The calibrated focal length is 41.1785. Calibration by: Alexandra Koh.

In recent years we have seen the arrival of affordable astro-CCD cameras and sophisticated computer-driven telescopes, and what was too expensive for the keen amateur astronomer only a few years ago is now within the financial means of many, although this still remains a highly expensive hobby!

Like the professionals, many amateurs have now replaced their film cameras with CCD imagers, mainly because they don't have to wait until the film is developed, but also because CCD offers something like the equivalent of 20 000 ISO speed, and its linear response allows accurate luminance measurements to be evaluated. Yet another advantage with CCD sensors is their lack of reciprocity failure, a problem common to photographic film, particularly in astronomy where long time exposures are necessary for recording faint stellar images.

A camera exposure of 1/50 second at $f/11$ provides the same exposure as 1/100 second at $f/8$ and, similarly, 1/30 second at $f/11$ should give the same exposure as 1/1000 second at $f/2$. This follows the so-called *reciprocity law,* which states that the product of radiation intensity ($I$), and exposure time ($t$), equals a constant.[60] This can be formally stated as:

$$It = \text{const.} \qquad (8.8)$$

But photographic materials are well known to deviate from this law, particularly colour films, either when exposure times are too short ($< 0.001$ second), or too long ($> 30$ seconds), with reciprocity limits depending on the type of film employed.[61][62] Fortunately CCD sensors obey the law pretty well in this respect.

A number of special CCD imagers are now available for astronomy. Some are designed for star tracking and others for recording; the latter are usually cooled to provide negligible dark current and low noise. It is important to remember that, in astronomy, exposures are usually counted in minutes or hours, and so system noise (dark current) has to be removed as much as possible.

Although modern telescopes can be connected to a computer that will find a given star on command, astrophotography requires accurate tracking as the earth moves during exposure. This can be done by following a reference star (in a field offset from the main field of interest) with a 'guidescope', and a drive corrector to keep this star centred while the telescope tracks on its equatorial mount.

For professional work accurate tracking can be accomplished with a CCD controller using fast framing rates, where the reference star is image-processed to allow the telescope to be controlled automatically over long exposure periods.[63]

AstroCam Ltd (a company specialising in astronomical cameras: see Appendix C) offer a large range of cooled CCD imagers which, although originally designed to meet the stringent requirements of astronomers recording faint stars and galaxies, are now being used for other applications in science.

Since cooled CCD systems enable extremely small differences of light intensity to be detected, details of very low contrast phenomena can be studied against much brighter backgrounds, without saturation of the higher intensity areas. As a consequence, cooled CCD cameras far surpass most other imaging systems in their ability to detect low contrast images with high sensitivity and wide dynamic range.

AstroCam produce a family of cooled CCD cameras in their Capella and Antares range of imagers which, apart from all the traditional benifits of cooled CCD systems, offer high-speed readout capabilities at very low noise levels. The Capella and Antares products differ mainly with respect to the read-out rates at which they operate, with the Capella range being the faster system.

Three models in the Capella family are available, providing a choice of grey-level resolution and speed:

- basic Capella system provides a 12 bit resolution (4096 grey levels) at pixel rates from 500 KHz to 8 MHz,
- Capella Beta gives 14 bit digitisation (16 384 grey levels) at up to 2 MHz,
- Capella Beta+ gives 14 bit digitisation up to 5 MHz.

Typically, each Capella system comprises three basic components: a cooled CCD camera head, an electronics unit, and Imager 2 camera control with software. Two types of cooled head are available: air cooled or liquid cooled. The air cooled system employs thermoelectric (Peltier) primary cooling with air cooled heat-exchangers, and the liquid cooled system is the same, except that it uses water cooled heat-exchangers.

Peltier cooled camera heads consist of a number of junctions between two dissimilar materials so that, when a current is passed in the correct direction through these junctions, localised cooling occurs. This has the effect of cooling the CCD imager mounted within the sealed cooling compartment.

It is common practice to cool astro-CCD imagers in order to reduce the amount of thermally generated dark current as explained in Chapter 4 and quantified by Eq: 4.10. Accumulation of dark current severely limits the performance of uncooled systems but, by lowering the temperature of the sensor, dark current is reduced by a factor of about 10 for every 20 °C drop in CCD temperature. However, cooling below −140 °C gives no further advantage since at these temperatures CCDs no longer function properly.

The AstroCam TE3/A camera head incorporates a Peltier/Air cooling system, whereas the TE3/W incorporates a Peltier/Liquid system, both of which offer a limiting luminance sensitivity of $10^{-9}$ lux. Both of these systems can be attached to either Pentax or Nikon cameras, by either screw or bayonet mounts.[64]

For the ultimate in sensitivity and dynamic range, a liquid-nitrogen cooled CCD head is the best answer. With these systems dark current can be reduced to less than one electron per pixel per hour by cooling to approximately −140 °C, and dynamic range can be extended to $10^5 : 1$ within a single exposure. The AstroCam Compact LN/C head can meet these specifications and also provide a limiting luminance sensitivity as low as $10^{-11}$ lux. Liquid-nitrogen cooled heads contain the imager within a vacuum sealed housing to minimise heat loss, with the CCD chip connected by a *cold finger* to a container filled with liquid nitrogen. The user can then select and stabilise the operating temperature within the range −60 °C to −140 °C.

## *CCDs for astronomy*

A good variety of CCDs is available for astronomical work, and can be selected according to the user's requirements. Well-known suppliers are AstroCam,[65] Hamamatsu,[66] SBIG,[67] Celestron[68] and Starlight Xpress,[69] all of which supply cooled imaging units and guidance systems.

The Santa Barbara Imaging Group (SBIG) have combined imaging and auto-guidance in their ST-7 and ST-8 self-guiding imaging cameras that contain two CCD detectors: one for guiding, the other for collecting the image. This allows the imaging CCD to integrate while the PC uses the guiding CCD to correct the telescope. Both these models use a Kodak CCD detector with 9 μm square pixels, and carefully guided exposures of one hour are possible, enabling a standard Celstron C-8 telescope to capture nineteenth magnitude stars.* Specifications for these models are shown in Table: 8.2.

*Table 8.2*

|  | **SBIG Model ST-7** | **SBIG Model ST-8** |
|---|---|---|
| Resolution | 765 × 510 pixels | 1534 × 1020 pixels |
| Total pixels | 390 0001 | 1 500 000 |
| CCD area | 6.9 × 4.6 mm | 13.8 × 9.2 mm |
| Celestron C-8 f.o.v | 12 × 8 arc minutes | 24 × 16 arc minutes |
| Software | Windows and MSDOS | Windows and MSDOS |
| Colour filter wheel | CFW-8 | CFW-8 |

* Apparent steller magnitudes are based on an empirical system where a magnitude of six is just visible to the naked eye. Stars that are below the visible threshold have a magnitude greater than six. This system was evolved many years ago (second century BC) when stars were categorised with brightnesses on a scale from 1 to 100, in six brightness groups. In this logarithmic system, a second magnitude star such as the North Star (Polaris) is 2.51 times fainter than a first magnitude star, and so on. Stars brighter than zero magnitude (Vega), have a negative value, such as Sirius (–1.42) the brightest star in the sky.

AstroCam supply a range of CCDs with a great variety of pixel numbers, pixel sizes and sensitivities. Standard CCDs all show similar spectral sensitivities between 400 nm and 1000 nm. However, special techniques can be used to increase the spectral sensitivity.

## *Thinned CCDs*

Thinned CCDs are treated so that the side away from the electrodes is mechanically and chemically etched to an overall thickness of only 10–15 μm. The device is then mounted so that incident radiation falls on the rear surface of the CCD, and does not have to pass through the covering electrodes (as with the configuration shown in Fig. 4.8). As a consequence blue-wavelength sensitivity is enhanced, and sensitivity to other wavelengths improved. Thinned CCDs may also be coated with AstroCam's Astrochrome 90, which further enhances ultra-violet sensitivity down to 180 nm or, without the standard fused silica window, down to 90 nm! Astrochrome 90 is available for all types of CCD.

There are a good number of CCD manufacturers and these are heavily represented in astronomy where it can be argued the CCD has had the greatest impact in terms of opening up new research possibilities. Characteristics of some of these CCDs are listed in Table 8.3.

*Table 8.3.*

| CCD | CCD15-11* | KAF – 1600 | CCD 442 |
|---|---|---|---|
| Manufacturer | EEV | Kodak | Loral |
| Pixel format (H × V) | 256 × 1024 | 1536 × 1024 | 2048 × 2048 |
| Sensitive Area (mm) | 6.9 × 27.6 | 13.8 × 9.2 | 30 × 30 |
| Pixel Size (μm) | 27 × 27 | 9 × 9 | 15 × 15 |
| Typical full-well capacity (electrons) | 600 000 | 85 000 | 400 000 |
| Typical read noise (electrons) at 40 kHz | 4 | 8 | 6 |
| Typical dark signal (e /px /s) | 0.03 – 0.3 | 0.05 | 10** |

* Standard or thinned. ** Dark signals will be reduced when using thermoelectric cooled heads.

## *CCD astronomy in practice*

The CCD is clearly an essential component of modern astronomical instrumentation, as proved by both professional and amateur alike. In the professional theatre we have the Hubble Space Telescope using CCDs to achieve high resolution from space, and ground-based astronomers developing techniques of 'adaptive optics' whereby distortions introduced by the atmosphere can be corrected in certain instances to allow a dramatic increase in image sharpness.[69]

A good example of what can be done with modern optical techniques is the new Cambridge Optical Aperture Synthesis Telescope (COAST), which is designed to generate diffraction limited images with a resolution as good as one milliarc second. Consisting of four telescopes on separate foundations, COAST feeds beams from the same object to a central laboratory where the beams are combined.[70]

For the four beams to interfere with optimum fringe visibility each telescope must be accurately and continually aligned to remove apparent first-order shift of the images caused by the atmosphere. These adjustments must be made at rates in excess of 100 Hz, and are realised by using a fast detector system namely the EEV CCD15-11 (EEV Ltd, Chelmsford, UK).

A good example of COAST imagery can be seen in Fig. 8.16 (see colour section) which shows successive CCD records of the binary star Capella. An interesting subject, and one of the brightest stars visible (apparent magnitude 0.08), Capella is nearly 50 light years away and can be found in the constellation of Auriga (RA 5 h 16.6', dec +46° 00'). In Fig. 8.16, Capella's two resolved bodies (separated by 55 milliarc seconds) are shown rotating around each other in successive exposures.

The COAST system is obviously very professional and also very expensive, but serious work continues to be done by amateurs using relatively inexpensive equipment. Many examples are shown regularly in magazines such as *Astronomy Now*, where numerous CCD images are printed with full details. Typical examples include deep-sky subjects such as galaxies, which are regularly exposed by amateur astronomers using off-the-shelf equipment such as the Starlight Xpress SXL8 CCD camera.

The Starlight Xpress SXL8 is a frame transfer CCD imager with a 7.7 $mm^2$ sensitive area providing an array of $512 \times 512$ pixels, each 15 $\mu m^2$. This camera head can be supplied in either Standard Grade (with a few minor blemishes) or Super Grade which is essentially perfect. However, published results taken with the Standard Grade imager show that this low-cost version (£790) is suitable for most workers. Images of planetary nebula, such as the Dumbell (M27), are easily recorded using a 160 second exposure with an $f/4.3$, 330 mm telescope. Similarly, it has been shown that, with the same system, very faint subjects like the Hercules globular cluster (M13) can be successfully recorded with only an 80 second exposure. Some idea of the light grasp involved can be appreciated when one considers that M13 is at the limit of naked eye visibility (with an apparent magnitude of 5.9), and is only obvious on a clear night. Found in the northern hemisphere, M13 is approximately 17 arc minutes in diameter and 23 000 light years away.

## 8.9 Scientific Laboratory Applications of Digital Imagers

Just as photography has long been an indispensable tool of science, so we find digital cameras are now taking over from film in a number of areas. This isn't to say that film has been discarded—far from it—but CCD imagers fit nicely into a number of high-tech systems now being introduced into modern laboratories, particularly where high resolution is not of paramount importance.

Among a variety of laboratory applications, the CCD camera can be found as an integral part of a number of screened-image systems. The camera then records the screen display and sends it direct to computer store, from where it can be processed with various types of software.

Hamamatsu, AstroCam and Kodak are among many firms that supply scientific CCD cameras for this expanding market. From Hamamatsu there is the Cooled C4880 series of cameras which couple high sensitivity with low noise and high dynamic range. A signal-to-noise ratio of 60 dB is claimed for this camera, with over 20 different models within the series. From Kodak there is the Megaplus

Camera Model 1.4, which has been specially developed for scientific image capture, including time-lapse photography, machine vision and diagnostic imaging. Full details on all these cameras can be obtained from the suppliers listed in Appendix C.

### X-Ray recording

Typical X-ray screen applications include the recording of X-ray diffraction images, formed from an X-ray image intensifier (with beryllium window); X-ray fluoroscopy (via an X-ray scintillator screen); Neutron radiography (where the neutron image is made visible by a neutron scintillator screen); and X-ray film imaging (simply recording conventional X-rays made on film). With all these applications a CCD imager has the distinct advantage of both linearity and wide dynamic range, which are essential attributes for recording images that can host a density range ($\Delta D$) as high as five or more.

Conversion from X-rays to visual photons is accomplished by scintillation screens, which commonly are made of zinc cadmium sulphide, or gadolinium oxisulphide, which are then imaged by a cooled CCD head fitted with fast (*f*/1.0) lenses.[71]

Since CCDs are sensitive to X-radiation it is also possible to employ CCD cameras for direct X-ray recording. In this case the imager has a Be (beryllium) window, and images in soft X-ray regions (100 eV and higher) can easily be acquired. In addition, X-ray energy can be determined by measuring the charge generated by a single quantum of X-radiation.

## *Spectrography*

Spectrography embraces most sciences and is routine procedure in many laboratories. The CCD camera is ideal for recording spectrographs since it offers a full spectral range, high sensitivity and linearity. In addition, the camera system is directly coupled to computer and software for data storage and analysis.

AstroCam supply a number of cameras and CCD chips for this purpose, employing their usual range of Capella and Antares systems. In addition they also market a specialist system dedicated to spectrography, known as the Prisma, which comes with a wide range of cooling options and choice of CCD chips. Prisma also has its own software (PrismaSoft) which operates in Windows 95 and offers complete spectral analysis and databasing functions.

For high-speed spectroscopy *frame transfer* chips are recommended because no mechanical shutter is required, and the time needed to operate a mechanical shutter can easily limit fast frame rates. Small shutters, as used in the AstroCam TE3 heads, cannot be used for exposures smaller than 10 ms, whereas frame transfer CCDs can always be gathering light during the period when the stored charges are read out. However, with the Capella family of AstroCam imagers only the EEV CCD37 is available in frame transfer mode; it can be operated with one microsecond parallel transfer times. With a *fast read* Capella head, the system is capable of recording up to 127 transient spectroscopic events (images) at intervals of 8 μs, using the EEV CCD37 chip.

Perhaps one of the most significant advances in CCD spectroscopy is due to the researches of Professor David Batchelder (Leeds University), who constructed a CCD system for Raman spectroscopy in the early 1990s. In the past a typical Raman spectrum (due to light being scattered by vibration of atoms in a sample) would take several hours to obtain, but with new optical filters, improved optical design, and CCD detectors, measurements take only seconds for most semiconductor and polymer applications.[72]

## *Optical transmission microscopy*

Transmission microscopy covers traditional options such as brightfield, darkfield, phase contrast, interference contrast, and fluorescent techniques. But apart from brightfield illumination, all these methods involve varying degrees of light loss which, at high magnifications, can make film recording very difficult. A common problem with biological specimens is their inherent low contrast and, although counter-staining can produce artificial enhancement, not all specimens can be treated in this fashion, which means that special low-light options have to be employed.

The introduction of cooled high-resolution CCD cameras has improved matters considerably. First of all, their greater sensitivity allows low-light-level imagery to be recorded with ease, and secondly it is possible to enhance contrast either by software or, with cameras like those in the Hamamatsu C2400 series,[73] within the circuitry of the Argus-20 Image Processor.[74]

These CCD camera features provide considerable advantage over film, and make it possible to obtain high-quality images from specimens so low in contrast that they were previously unobservable. This is particularly the case with differential interference contrast microscopy, as shown in Fig. 8.17, and also with fluorescence microscopy.

## Transmission electron microscopy

Both Hamamatsu and AstroCam provide cooled CCD systems for transmission electron microscopy (TEM), both of which employ standard CCD cameras to capture a TEM image displayed on the instrument's scintillation (conversion) screen. The conversion screen is situated inside the vacuum chamber of the TEM so that image electrons can be converted to photons, which are then recorded by the CCD camera.

*Fig. 8.17* Low contrast microscopic subject (fly's wing), imaged by differential interference microscopy, and recorded with a scientific CCD camera. Image courtesy of AstroCam Ltd, Cambridge Science Park.

The conversion screen is a single thin sheet (0.5 mm thick) of yttrium aluminium garnet (YAG), and the CCD head is usually fitted with an $f/1.0$ lens focused to the front surface of the YAG screen.

## 8.10 Freelance Photography

Finally, among literally hundreds of applications one could mention, it seems appropriate to end this chapter with what must be one of the most well-known, and perhaps exciting areas of imaging: that of the freelance photographer. It is particularly important given the alarming prediction made at the 1996 Photokina (Köln) exhibition that, by 1998, half of the freelance photographers would be out of work as a result of digital technology!

In an interesting article by Martin Evening in *Image* (the magazine of the Association of Photographers), the writer says that, in the future, it may become harder to define the difference between a photographer and an illustrator.[75] And that photographers will, out of necessity, have to invest in digital equipment: digital capture, modem/ISDN connections, etc.

As Martin Evening sums up so elegantly, when speaking on behalf of freelance workers: 'Digital technology has the potential to speed up the production process; time and money can be saved by taking full advantage of electronic communications. As with the cinema industry, it is not going to be the photographers who decide whether digital technology has a future or not—it will be the people buying our services.'

## 8.11 Conclusions

Chapter 8 illustrates a representative sample of digital imaging applications and, although most of the emphasis has been devoted to scientific and technical work, this was more to emphasise potential and diversity rather than anything else.

For professional photographers the image is the thing! And in their highly subjective business, artistry and originality are essential qualities, regardless of the medium employed. At a price, it seems that digital systems are now being accepted for quality work in product photography, portraiture, fashion and advertising. But success in this work goes beyond the technical and, provided that digital cameras can equal the photographic quality expected by their clients, the rest stands or falls on pure commercial grounds.

On the other hand, for the casual user, amateur, desk-top publisher, technologist or scientist, digital systems (and associated software) offer convenience, speed, economy and technical expertise handed on a plate! With a little perseverance anyone can master both computer and software, and produce images of a standard otherwise impossible to achieve outside an extensive course in photography.

There can be no doubt that CCD imagers are here to stay! And although sensor technology may shift from CCD to complementary metal oxide semiconductor (CMOS) in the near future, we can expect further innovations and more use of these cameras as they increase in quality and decrease in cost. Certainly we can look forward to some drastic price cutting as market competition increases; and as cameras, computers and software approach more attractive levels, so will digital imagery become as normal as photography was yesterday!

# Appendix A  Binary and ASCII Codes

## Binary code

Like decimal notation, the binary system of numbering is a positional notation, where the value of a binary number depends not only on the bits it contains, but also tier position in the number. The positional value increases from right to left by powers of 2, as the following list makes clear.

| Decimal No. | Powers of 2 | Binary No. |
|---|---|---|
| 0 | $(0 \times 2^0)$ | 0000 |
| 1 | $(1 \times 2^0)$ | 0001 |
| 2 | $(1 \times 2^1)$ | 0010 |
| 3 | $(1 \times 2^1) + (1 \times 2^0)$ | 0011 |
| 4 | $(1 \times 2^2)$ | 0100 |
| 5 | $(1 \times 2^2) + (0 \times 2^1) + (1 \times 2^0)$ | 0101 |
| 6 | $(1 \times 2^2) + (1 \times 2^1) + (0 \times 2^0)$ | 0110 |
| 7 | $(1 \times 2^2) + (1 \times 2^1) + (1 \times 2^0)$ | 0111 |
| 8 | $(1 \times 2^3)$ | 1000 |
| 9 | $(1 \times 2^3) + (0 \times 2^2) + (0 \times 2^1) + (1 \times 2^0)$ | 1001 |
| 10 | $(1 \times 2^3) + (0 \times 2^2) + (1 \times 2^1) + (0 \times 2^0)$ | 1010 |
| 11 | $(1 \times 2^3) + (0 \times 2^2) + (1 \times 2^1) + (1 \times 2^0)$ | 1011 |
| 12 | $(1 \times 2^3) + (1 \times 2^2) + (0 \times 2^1) + (0 \times 2^0)$ | 1100 |
| 15 | $(1 \times 2^3) + (1 \times 2^2) + (1 \times 2^1) + (1 \times 2^0)$ | 1111 |
| 16 | $(1 \times 2^4)$ | 10000 |
| 20 | $(1 \times 2^4) + (0 \times 2^3) + (1 \times 2^2) + (0 \times 2^1) + (0 \times 2^0)$ | 10100 |
| 32 | $(1 \times 2^5)$ | 100000 |
| 100 | $(1 \times 2^6) + (1 \times 2^5) + (0 \times 2^4) + (0 \times 2^3) + (1 \times 2^2) + (0 \times 2^1) + (0 \times 2^0)$ | 1100100 |

In order to convert from binary to decimal we multiply each bit in the binary number by the power of 2 with the least significant bit (on extreme right) having the positional value of $2^0$, then add them all together. In the above examples (see under power of 2) we can see that the coefficient of each term is either a one or a zero and it is the coefficents that make up the binary number. Thus, for decimal 20, we add (from the right) as: $0 + 0 + (1 \times 2^2) + 0 + (1 \times 2^4)$ which sums to $4 + 16 = 20$.

# ASCII Code

Binary digits (bits) can also be used to represent letters of the alphabet, numbers and punctuation marks. One such 7 bit code is the ASCII (American Standard Code for Information Interchange) which is used extensively in small computer systems to translate from the keyboard chracters to computer language. Since this code represents letters as well as numbers it is known as an *alphanumeric code*.

| Character | ASCII | Character | ASCII |
|-----------|---------|-----------|---------|
| 0 | 0110000 | A | 1000001 |
| 1 | 0110001 | B | 1000010 |
| 2 | 0110010 | C | 1000011 |
| 3 | 0110011 | D | 1000100 |
| 4 | 0110100 | E | 1000101 |
| 5 | 0110101 | F | 1000110 |
| 6 | 0110110 | G | 1000111 |
| 7 | 0110111 | H | 1001000 |
| 8 | 0111000 | I | 1001001 |
| 9 | 0111001 | J | 1001010 |
|   |         | K | 1001011 |
|   |         | L | 1001100 |
|   |         | M | 1001101 |
|   |         | N | 1001110 |
|   |         | O | 1001111 |
|   |         | P | 1010000 |
|   |         | Q | 1010001 |
|   |         | R | 1010010 |
|   |         | S | 1010011 |
|   |         | T | 1010100 |
|   |         | U | 1010101 |
|   |         | V | 1010110 |
|   |         | W | 1010111 |
|   |         | X | 1011000 |
|   |         | Y | 1011001 |
|   |         | Z | 1011010 |

# Appendix B Fundamental Constants and Conversion of Units

## Fundamental Constants

| Constant | Symbol | Value |
|----------|--------|-------|
| Velocity of light | $c$ | $2.999\ 925 \times 10^8$ m s$^{-1}$ |
| Boltzmann constant | $k$ | $1.380\ 622 \times 10^{-23}$ JK$^{-1}$ |
| Charge of electron | $e$ | $1.602\ 191\ 7 \times 10^{-19}$ C |
| Rest mass of electron | $m_e$ | $9.109\ 5 \times 10^{-31}$ kg |
| Permittivity of free space | $\varepsilon_0$ | $8.854\ 185\ 3 \times 10^{-12}$ Mm$^{-1}$ |
| Planck constant | $h$ | $6.626\ 196 \times 10^{-34}$ Js |
| Mechanical equivalent of light | $M$ | $1.47$ mW Lm$^{-1}$ |

## Conversion Factors

| Length | m | cm | mm | $\mu$m | nm | inch | feet |
|--------|---|----|----|--------|----|------|------|
| 1 metre | 1 | 100 | 100 | $10^6$ | $10^9$ | 39.3701 | 3.280 84 |

| Length | km | mile | nautical mile |
|--------|-----|------|---------------|
| 1 km | 1 | 0.621 371 | 0.539 957 |
| 1 mile | 1.609 34 | 1 | 0.868 976 |
| 1 naut. mile | 1.852 | 1.150 78 | 1 |

| Velocity | ms$^{-1}$ | kmh$^{-1}$ | mph |
|----------|-----------|------------|-----|
| 1 metre per second | 1 | 3.6 | 2.236 94 |
| 1 km per hour | 0.277 78 | 1 | 0.621 371 |
| 1 mph | 0.44704 | 1.609 344 | 1 |

# Appendix C Manufacturers and Agents, Institutions and Publications

## Manufacturers and Agents

Adobe Systems (UK) Ltd, Hampshire House, Wade Road, Basingstoke, Hants RG24 8PL. Tel: (01256) 463344. Fax: (01256) 847163.

Agfa-Gevaert Ltd, 27 Great West Road, Brentford, Middx TW8 9AX. Tel: (0181) 231420. Fax: (0181) 231457.

Apple Computer (UK) Ltd, 6 Roundwood Avenue, Stockley Park, Uxbridge UB11 1BB. FreePhone: (0800) 127753.

Arc/Info, GIS Consultants, ESRI (UK), 23 Woodford Road, Watford WD1 1PB. Tel: (01923) 210450.

AstroCam Ltd, Innovation Centre, Cambridge Science Park, Milton Road, Cambridge CB4 4GS. Tel: (01223) 420705. Fax: (01223) 423021.

Canon (UK) Ltd, Brent Trading Centre, North Circular Road, London NW10 0JF. Tel: (0181) 459 1266. Fax: (0181) 459 4202.

Comstock (Stock Photography), 28 Chelsea Wharf, 15 Lots Road, London SW10 0YY. Tel: (0171) 351 4448. Fax: (0171) 352 8414.

Digital Darkroom, West Park, Silsoe, Bedfordshire. Tel/Fax: (01525) 862456. E-mail: Digital Darkroom@.MSN.COM.

Fuji Photo Film (UK) Ltd, Fuji Film House, 125 Finchley Road, London NW3 6JH. Tel: (0181) 367 3560. Fax: (0181)367 6384.

Hamamatsu Photonics (UK) Ltd, Lough Point, 2 Gladbeck Way, Windmill Hill, Enfield EN2 7JA. Tel: (0181) 367 3560. Fax: (0181) 367 6384.

Hewlett Packard, Cain Road, Bracknell, Berkshire RG12 1HN. Tel: (01344) 369222.

John Bigglestone and Company. The Wharf Studio Couch Lane, Devizes SN10 1EB.

Kodak Ltd, Digital and Applied Imaging, PO Box 66, Station Road, Hemel Hempstead, Herts HP1 1JU. Tel: (01442) 845228. Fax: (01442) 845113.

Minolta (UK) Ltd, Rooksley Park, Precedent Drive, Rooksley, Milton Keynes MK13 8HF. Tel: (01908) 200400. Fax: (01908) 200391.

Nikon (UK) Ltd, Nikon House, 380 Richmond Road, Kingston-upon-Thames, Surrey KT2 5PR. Tel: (0181) 541 4440. Fax: (0181) 541 4584.

Pro Digital Imaging, South Point, South Accommodation Road, Leeds LS10 1PP. Tel: (0113) 245 4848. Fax: (0113) 4848.

Sony, Brian Reece Scientific Ltd, 12 West Mills, Newbury, Berkshire RG14 5HG. Tel: (01653) 32827. Fax: (01635) 34542.

Synoptics Ltd, 271 Cambridge Science Park, Milton Road, Cambridge CB4 4WE. Tel: (01223) 423223. Fax: (01223) 4200020.

Vision Corporation Ltd, Talmin House, Hogwood Business Park, Ivanhoe Road, Wokingham, Berks RG11 4QQ. Tel: (01734) 730911. Fax: (01734) 730910.

## Institutions

Bath Spa University College (RSGIS Unit), Newton Park, Newton St Loe, Bath BA2 9BN. Tel: (01225) 8735580. Fax: (01225) 875776.

British Institute of Professional Photography, Fox Talbot House, Amwell End, Ware, Herts SG12 9HN. Tel: (01920) 464011. Fax: (01920) 487056.

Mac/Windows Academy (UK), Gloucester House, Woodside Lane, London N12 8TP. (Photoshop training). Tel: (0181) 445 5225. Fax: (0181) 446 3314.

NESCOT, Nescot Epsom Centre, Longmead Road, Epsom, Surrey KT19 9BH. (Digital imaging courses). Tel: (0181) 394 3176. Fax: (0181) 394 3232.

University College London, Gower Street, London WC1E 6BT. Tel: (0171) 387 7050. Fax: (0171) 380 0453.

University of Newcastle-upon-Tyne, Department of Geomatics, Newcastle-upon-Tyne NE1 7RU. Tel: (0191) 222 6000.

## Publications

*Advanced Imaging*, 445 Broad Hollow Road, Melville, NY 11747, USA. Tel: (516) 845 2700. Fax: (516) 845 2797.

*Computer Arts*, Future Publishing Ltd, Somerton, Somerset TA11 6BR. Tel: (01225) 822 511.

*Electronic Imaging*, Market Link Publishing Ltd, The Mill, Bearwalden Business Park, Wendens Ambro, Saffron Walden, Essex CB11 4JX. Tel: (01799) 544200.

*Scientific Computing World*, Institute of Physics Circulation Centre, WDIS Publishing House, Victoria Road, Ruislip, Middx HA4 0SX. Tel: (0181) 845 8545.

# Glossary

**absolute temperature** thermodynamic temperature expressed in units of Kelvin. Zero degrees on this scale (absolute zero) represents the lowest temperature theoretically possible, and is the temperature at which the kinetic energy of atoms and molecules is minimal. Absolute zero = 273 °C.

**A/D converter** a device that converts continuously varying analogue signals into discrete digital signals or numbers.

**Adobe Photoshop** well-known and very popular imaging software for Mac and PC computers.

**Aldus Photostyler** now taken over by Adobe and no longer available, this remains an excellent image-processing program (replaced by Photoshop).

**algorithm** a rule for solving a mathematical problem in a finite number of steps.

**aliasing** an effect in computer graphics and bit-mapped images, where diagonal lines, curves or circles produce a stair-stepped appearance when resolution is too coarse.

**alphanumeric** consisting of letters, numbers, spaces and other characters (see ASCII).

**analogue** any device that represents changing values by a continuously variable physical property, such as voltage in a circuit. An analogue device can manage an infinite set of values within its range, whereas a digital device can only manage a fixed number of values.

**analogue display** a video display (such as VGA) is capable of a continuous range of grey levels or colours. By comparison, a digital display can only resolve a finite range of greys or colours (such as the old EGA system).

**ASCII** acronym for American Standard Code for Information Interchange. This standard code assigns numeric values to letters, numbers, punctuation marks and control characters, to provide compatibility between computers and peripherals.

**bandwidth** in communications and optics, bandwidth refers to the range between highest and lowest frequency (or wavelength) available for transmission.

**binary** a term reserved for any system that uses two different states, components, conditions or conclusions. In mathematics the binary system uses combinations of the digits 0 and 1 to represent all values.

**binary numbers** numbers stored in binary form (see Appendix A).

**bit** contraction of binary digit. A bit is the basic unit of information in a binary system of numbering, where 0 equals off and 1 equals on. Bits can be grouped to make up larger units, such as the byte, where 8 bits equal one byte.

**bit-mapped graphics** an image created by a series of dots (pixels), rather than a set of lines (vectors). Bit-mapped graphics consume large amounts of disk and memory space.

**black-body radiation** electromagnetic radiation (EMR) emitted by a hypothetical body that absorbs all the radiation falling on it. It thus has 100% absorptance and emissivity. The nearest practical approach to a black-body radiator is a small hole in the wall of an enclosure at uniform temperature.

**brightness** a subjective term that describes the sensation of light entering the eye. Roughly related to the objective term luminance, which is a physical unit.

**buffer** an area of memory used for temporary storage of data.

**byte** a contraction of the term binary digit eight. A byte is a group of eight bits that usually holds a single character. Bytes are further grouped into kilobytes (1024 bytes), megabytes (1 048 576 bytes), or gigabytes (1 073 741 824 bytes).

**C** a compiled programming language developed for professional programmers. Useful for writing programs that are fast, powerful and capable of being moved from one computer to another without difficulty.

**C++** an object oriented version of C. Object oriented programming (OOP) views a program as a set of self-contained objects that interact with others by passing messages between them.

**CAD** computer-aided design.

**calibration** a term used in photogrammetry to define a metric camera (which has its focal length and image radial distortions calibrated to an exacting value). A calibrated camera is essential for topographic mapping.

**CCD** charge coupled device. A solid state imaging sensor that uses an array of metal oxide semiconductors (MOS) to produce an electrical output proportional to the amount of light (EMR) incident upon each picture element (pixel). Each signal charge is clocked-out to the output register by coupling all adjacent cells. Analogue signals then undergo A/D conversion to create a digital image.

**CD-ROM** acronym for compact disk–read only memory. A high-capacity (650 Mb) optical storage device used to store large image files, dictionaries, encyclopaedias, etc.

**CFA interpolation** colour filter array interpolation. Algorithm for improving a CCD colour image by using 'cross talk' between an array of coloured filters.

**charge packets** an optically induced signal charge stored in the potential well of each CCD storage element (pixel).

**CIE system** an internationally accepted system (Commission Internationale de l'Éclairage) for defining colour in terms of a modified triangle which contains all spectral colours. In the CIE system the three primary colours (red, green, blue) are designated X, Y, Z, thus a colour can be located within the locus of the triangle by quoting any two graph coordinates to find hue and saturation, while luminance (brightness) is provided by an additional value.

**CMOS** complementary metal oxide semiconductor.

**CMYK** cyan, magenta, yellow and black. The four colours used in printing, where CMY are the complementary colours.

**conductor** a substance or body that offers little resistance to the flow of an electric current.

**D/A converter** a device that will convert a digital signal into an analogue one.

**dark current** thermally generated electrical noise in a CCD imaging system.

**decibel** unit used to compare two power levels. Two power levels, $P$ and $P_o$ differ by $n$ decibels when $n = 10 \log_{10}(P/P_o)$.

**dielectric** a substance that is capable of sustaining electrical stress, that is, an insulator.

**digital** a term that describes any system that represents values in the form of binary digits (binary codes consisting of 0s and 1s)

**DOS** acronym for disk operating system.

**DVD** a high-density version compact disk. DVD increases optical disk capacity from the normal 650 Mb to 4.7 Gb (gigabytes) by using double tracks on both sides of the disk.

**electronvolt** a unit of energy (symbol eV) equal to the work done on an electron when it moves through a potential difference of one volt.

**frame-grabber** a device that converts a video image into digital form suitable for computer display. Sometimes called a video digitiser, most frame-grabbers can be attached to any video system producing an RGB signal.

**full-frame transfer** a CCD imager that employs its full array of pixels for imaging, in contrast to the frame transfer types, which employ half the total CCD elements for imaging and half for temporary storage.

**grey scale** a term used in computer graphics (grey levels) to describe a series of shades from white through any number of grey levels to black. The number of grey levels available depends on the number of bits dedicated to each pixel. Thus, a pixel with 8 bits (one byte) has $2^8 = 256$ grey levels.

**ground state** the state of a system (an atom for example) in its lowest energy level, in contrast to its excited state.

**halftone** when an original photograph is printed through a (halftone) screen, the image is broken up into a pattern of dots. Dark areas form dense dot patterns that can merge together, whereas highlight areas have few dots.

**high pass filter** an image processing operation which employs a mathematical 'filter' to provide image sharpening or edge enhancement when applied to the digital image array. A particular example is the Laplacian filter.

**HSB** acronym for hue, saturation and brightness, which are the three main attributes of any colour (HSB is also a colour model used in computer graphics). Hue is the name of the colour, saturation is how pure the colour may be (freedom from other colours), and brightness refers to its visual luminance.

**illuminance** a photometric unit (symbol E). The light shining from a source onto a scene or subject.

**image-processing** the computer processing of a graphical image, made possible by the use of various software packages dedicated to image enhancement and over-all control of the image.

**insulator** a substance that is a poor conductor of electricity due to a lack of mobile electrons.

**ISO** International Standards Organisation (based in Geneva), establishes world-wide standards in numerous fields, such as photography (film-speeds), and computer communications.

**JPEG** Joint Photographic Experts Group. A well-known image compression standard and file format. JPEG employs lossy compression methods, achieves compression ratios as high as 20 : 1 and stores 24 bit colour images.

**LCD** liquid crystal display. Usually found in portable computers (laptop and notebook) where display screen technology employs an electric current to to align crystals in a special liquid.

**LED** light emitting diode.

**lightness** lightness is the continuum running from a white to a black surface, and should not be confused with brightness. Whereas a grey cat in sunlight and the same cat in the shade will be of equal lightness (if constancy is perfect), in sunlight the cat will appear much brighter.

**low-pass filter** commonly known as a smoothing filter, a low-pass filter is generally used to remove image noise and speckle.

**luminance** the objective correlate of brightness (symbol L), luminance is a measure of how much light is coming from a surface. The unit of luminance is the candle/square metre ($Cd\ m^2$).

**LUT** look-up table. A collection of data values.

**menu** a list of commands, or options, available in the displayed software.

**MOS** metal oxide semiconductor. The individual light-sensitive elements that make up a CCD.

**Munsell system** a practical system for designating a colour, in terms of hue, saturation and value (brightness). The Munsell system can be purchased as a three-dimensional model (Munsell Tree) or in book form, with over 1200 colour samples.

**Nyquist limit** for a CCD sensor with pixel spatial frequency $k_s$, unambiguous resolution of image detail with a spatial frequency $k_i$, is not possible if $k_i > 0.5\ k_s$.

**OCR** optical character recognition. Computer recognition of printed matter.

**PCMCIA** PC Memory Card International Association. A standard for plug-in adaptors for portable computers and digital cameras.

**photo-electron** an electron emitted from a substance due to irradiation by EMR.

**photometry** the scientific study of visual radiation, where photometric quantities can be measured either by eye, or by photoelectric devices.

**pixel** contraction of picture element. The smallest element (resolution) of an image.

**potential well** signal information in a CCD element is carried in the form of a charge of electrons, localised under the electrode with the highest (positive) applied potential. This electric charge is said to be stored in a potential well.

**RAM** acronym for randon access memory. The principal memory system in a computer used for the operating system, application programs and data.

**resistance** symbol $R$. The ratio of the potential difference ($V$) across an electrical component, to the current ($I$) passing through it. Related to voltage and current through Ohm's law as: $R = V/I$.

**resolution** a measure of the ability of an imaging system to separate individual components of an image. Classical theory suggests that a diffraction limited lens can resolve two points separated by a distance ($r$) as: $r = 1.22\lambda N$, where $\lambda$ is the wavelength of light and $N$ the relative aperture of the lens. With digital cameras, resolution is expressed in terms of the number of pixels within a CCD array, and in printing as the number of dots per inch (dpi).

**RGB** red, green, blue; the three additive primary colours.

**ROM** acronym for read only memory.

**RS-232-C** a standard interface between computer and a peripheral. RS-232 uses either a 9-pin or 25-pin connector, the C denotes a third revision of the Recomended Standard.

**SCSI** acronym for small computer system interface (pronounced scuzzy). SCSI is often used to connect hard disks, tape drives, scanners, printers, CD-ROM drives and digital cameras, in fact any peripheral that involves mass storage of data.

**semiconductor** a material that is in-between a conductor and an insulator, and whose electrical properties can be precisely controlled by the addition of dopants (impurities). The most common semiconductors are silicon and germanium.

**SVGA** super video graphics display (an enhancement to the standard VGA) which can display at least 800 pixels horizontally and 600 pixels vertically.

**terabyte** a terabyte is equal to 1000 gigabytes ($2^{40}$), or 1 099 511 627 776 bytes.

**thumbnail** a very low-resolution digital image, used for library file purposes.

**TWAIN** not an acronym. A somewhat humorous term for explaining an interface that is technology without an interesting name.

**valency band** the outermost electrons of an atom (those responsible for chemical bonding) occupy the valency band of a solid. If the valency band is filled and there is a wide forbidden band between it and the next highest empty band, then the material is an insulator. However, if the valency band is not completely filled, or if it overlaps with a higher empty energy band, then there are vacant levels that electrons can enter and the material will be a good conductor. Most metals have this property.

# References

(1) Graham, R.W., The Optimum Photographic Representation of Brightnesses in Interior Scenes. pp. 105–117. Ph.D thesis, CNAA (1975).

(2) Stevens, J.C. and Stevens, S.S. *J. Opt. Soc. Amer.*, **53**(3), pp. 375–385 (1963).

(3) Hopkinson, R.G. *Architectural Physics: Lighting*, HMSO, London, pp. 324–351 (1963).

(4) Hunt, R.W.G. *J. Phot. Sci.*, **1**, pp. 149–158 (1953).

(5) Hurvich, L.M. and Jameson, D. *The Perception of Lightness and Darkness*, Allyn & Bacon Inc., Boston, pp. 62–64 (1966).

(6) Graham, R.W. The Optimum Photographic Representation of Brightnesses in Interior Scenes, *J. Phot. Sci.*, **27**(3), May/June (1979).

(7) Klein, E. *Ber. Bunsenges. Phys. Chemie.*, **80**, p. 1082 (1976).

(8) Metz, H.J., Ruchti, S. and Seidel, K. *J. Phot. Sci.*, **26**, pp. 229–233 (1978).

(9) *Kodak Data for Aerial Photography*. Eastman Kodak Co. 6th edn. (1992).

(10) Shannon, C.E. *Bell Systems Tech. J.*, **27**, p. 623 (1948).

(11) Brown, F.M., Hall, H.J. and Kosar, J. Photographic Systems for Engineers. *SPSE*, p. 99 (1966).

(12) Pearson, D.E. *Transmission and Display of Pictorial Information*, p. 115, Pentech Press, London (1975).

(13) Saxby, G. Practical Holography: Appendix 3 in *The Fourier Approach to Image Formation*. Prentice Hall, pp. 475–492 (1994).

(14) Graham, R.W. and Read, R.E. *Manual of Aerial Photography*, Focal Press, pp. 147–158 (1986). Also, *Manual of Aerial Photography*, 2nd edn.

(15) Konecny, G., Schuhe, W. and Wu, J. Investigations on the Interpretability of Images by Different Sensors and Platforms for Small Scale Mapping, *Proceedings ISPRS*, Comm. 1, Symposium, Canberra, pp. 11–22 (1982).

(16) Makarovic, B. and Tempfli, K. Digitising Images and Automatic Processing in Photogrammetry. *ITC Journal*, **1**, pp. 107–126 (1979).

(17) Kosonocky, W.F. and Sauer, D.J. The ABCs of CCDs. RCA Booklet *Charge Coupled Devices and Applications*, April (1981).

(18) Yang, E.S. *Microelectronic Devices*. McGraw Hill International Edition, p. 229 (1988).

(19) Yang, E.S. *Microelectronic Devices*. McGraw Hill International Division, p. 232 (1988).

(20) Crawley, G. The Solid State Still Camera and the Future. *B. J. Phot.* p. 1115, 30 October (1981).

(21) Mills, J.P. The Implementation of a Digital Photogrammetric System and its Applications in Civil Engineering. Ph.D thesis, University of Newcastle-upon-Tyne, p. 12 (1996).

(22) Shortis, M.R. and Beyer, H.A. Sensor Technology for Digital Photogrammetry and Machine Vision. *Close Range Photogrammetry and Machine Vision*, ed. K.B. Atkinson, Whittles Publishing, pp.120–121 (1996).

(23) Carnes, J.E. and Kosonocky, W.F. *Charge Coupled Devices and Applications*. RCA Publication, April (1981).

(24) Muller, R.S. and Kamins, T.I. *Device Electronics for Integrated Circuits*. 2nd edn. John Wiley & Sons, New York, pp. 411 (1986).

(25) Janesick, J.R., Elliott, T., Dingizian, A. et al. New Advancements in CCD Technology – Sub-Electron Noise and 4096 × 4096 Pixel CCDs. *Charge Coupled Devices and Solid State Optical Sensors, SPIE,* **1242**, pp. 223–227 (1990).

(26) Crawley, G. CCD in Solid State Video. *B. J. Phot.* 4th August (1972).

(27) Crawley, G. Sony Unveils Still Video Camera. *B. J. Phot.* 4th September (1981).

(28) Crawley, G. The Solid State Still Camera and the Future. *B. J. Phot.* 30th October (1981).

(29) Shortis, M.R. et al. Comparative Geometric Tests of Industrial & Scientific CCD Cameras Using Plumb Line and Test Range Calibrations. *International Archives of Photogrammetry and Remote Sensing*, **30**(5W1), pp. 53–59 (1995).

(30) Mills, J.P. The Implementation of a Digital Photogrammetric System and its Applications in Civil Engineering. Ph.D thesis, University of Newcastle-upon-Tyne, pp. 18–19 (1996).

(31) Tinsley, J. *Electronic Imaging*, pp. 45–48, July (1996).

(32) Tinsley. J. *Electronic Imaging*, pp. 19–24, September (1995).

(33) Standage, T. Scan with a wave of the hand. p. 3 Connected. *The Daily Telegraph*, 28 January (1997).

(34) Warner, W.S., Graham, R.W. and Read, R.E. *Small Format Aerial Photography*, Whittles Publishing, p. 12 (1996).

(35) Gulliver, B. *The Aerial Reconnaissance Co*. Obtainable from 6 Knowle Hill, Bodiam, Robertsbridge, E. Sussex, TN2 5UP, UK.

(36) Schowengerdt, R.A. *Techniques for Image Processing and Classification in Remote Sensing*. Orlando Florida, Academic Press (1983).

(37) Mather, P. *Computer Processing of Remotely Sensed Images*, John Wiley & Sons (1987).

(38) Schalkoff, R.J. *Digital Image Processing and Computer Vision*. John Wiley & Sons (1989).

(39) Pratt, W.K. *Digital Image Processing*. John Wiley & Sons, New York (1978).

(40) Ford, A.M., Jacobson, R.E. and Attridge, G.G. Effects of Image Compression on Image Quality. *J. Phot. Sci.*, **43**, pp. 52–57 (1995).

(41) Van Nes, F.L. Spatial Modulation Transfer in the Human Eye. *J. Opt. Soc. Am.*, **57** pp. 401–406 (1967).

(42) Tinsley, J. Jet Propelled. *Electronic Imaging*, p. 49, November (1995).

(43) Tinsley, J. Prime Example. *Electronic Imaging*. p. 44, August (1995).

(44) Warner, W.S., Graham, R.W. and Read, R.E. *Small Format Aerial Photography*. Whittles Publishing (1996).

(45) Stringham, A. GPS and Photo CD. *Earth Observation Magazine*, pp. 55–57, June (1994).

(46) Hamit, F. Desktop NDT Vibration Tests. *Advanced Imaging*, p. 42, May (1996).

(47) Graham, R.W. Holography. *Printing Technology*, pp. 11–32, **16**(1) April (1972).

(48) Graham, R.W. A Simple Power Density Meter for Holography. *J. Phot. Sci.*, **30**(3), May/June (1982).

(49) *The Sunday Times*, 4 August (1996).

(50) Linney, A.D. et al. Three Dimensional Visualization of Data on Human Anatomy: Diagnosis and Surgical Planning. *Journal of Audiovisual Media in Medicine*, **16** pp. 4–10 (1993).

(51) Personal communication from R. Thomson, National Technical Support Unit, Police Scientific Development Branch (PSDP), Woodcock Hill, Sandridge, St Albans, Herts AL4 9HQ, UK.

(52) Griffiths, P. In The Army Now. *Brit. J. Digital Imaging*, pp. 15–16 (British Institute of Professional Photographers), 18 September (1996).

(53) Thomson, G.H. Aerospace Report No. 5. *J. Phot. Sci.*, **43**, pp. 36–37 (1995).

(54) Mills, J.P., Newton, I. and Graham, R.W. Aerial Photography for Surveying Purposes with a High Resolution Small Format Digital Camera. *Photogrammetric Record,* **15**(88), pp. 575–587 (1996).

(55) Fryer, J.G. Recent Developments in Camera Calibration for Close Range Applications. *International Archives of Photogrammetry and Remote Sensing*, **29**(B5), pp. 594–599 (1992).

(56) Thomson, G.H. A Practical Method for Determining the Ground Sampled Distance in Small Scale Aerial Photography. *J. Phot. Sci.*, **42**, pp. 129–132 (1994).

(57) Graham, R.W. The ITC Multispectral Camera System with Respect to Crop Prognosis in Winter Wheat. *ITC Journal* **2**, pp. 235–254 (1980).

(58) Graham, R.W. Multispectral Photography in Remote Sensing. *Brit. J. Phot.*, pp. 23–25 (1992).

(59) Gavin, M. CCD Time Machines. *Astronomy Now*, pp. 15–16, September (1996).

(60) Jacobson, R.E., Ray, S. and Attridge, G.G. *The Manual of Photography*, 8th edn., Focal Press, pp. 187–189 (1988).

(61) Cox, R.J. *Photographic Sensitivity*, Academic Press, pp. 105–106 (1973).

(62) Todd, H.N. and Zakia, R.D. *Photographic Sensitometry*, Morgan & Morgan Inc., New York, pp. 95–105 (1969).

(63) AstroCam. *Astronomy Applications Guide to Cooled CCD Imaging Systems*. AstroCam Ltd., Cambridge Science Park, Cambridge CB4 4GS.

(64) AstroCam. *Camera Head Data Sheet and Selection Guide*. AstroCam Ltd., Cambridge Science Park, Cambridge CB4 4GS.

(65) AstroCam. *CCD Data Sheet and Selection Guide*. AstroCam Ltd., Cambridge Science Park, Cambridge CB4 4GS.

(66) Hamamatsu Photonics (UK) Ltd., 2 Gladbeck Way (see Appendix C).

(67) Santa Barbara Instrument Group (SBIG). PO Box 5047, 1482 East Valley Road, 33 Santa Barbara, CA 93150, USA.

(68) Celestron International, 2835 Columbia Street, Torrance, CA 9053, USA.

(69) Jorden, P. New Detectors for New Astronomy. *Physics World*, pp. 40–45, May (1994).

(70) Mackay, C.D. Fast CCD Controllers Optimise Telescope Images. *Laser Focus World*, May (1996).

(71) AstroCam. *X-Ray Applications Guide to Cooled CCD Imaging Systems*. AstroCam Ltd., Cambridge Science Park, Cambridge CB4 4GS.

(72) Pitt, G.D. A Revolution in Raman Spectroscopy. *Physics in Business*, no. 13, pp. 6–7, Institute of Physics, February (1997).

(73) Hamamatsu. *C2400 Series Cameras for Video Microscopy*. Hamamatsu Ltd. (see Appendix C).

(74) Hamamatsu. *Image Processing and Analysis System for Optical Microscopes*. Hamamatsu Ltd., (see Appendix C).

(75) Evening, M. Digital Futures. *Image* (see Appendix C), pp. 5–7, January (1997).

# Index